James Barnes

Commodore Bainbridge

From the Gunroom to the Quarter-Deck

James Barnes

Commodore Bainbridge
From the Gunroom to the Quarter-Deck

ISBN/EAN: 9783337017989

Printed in Europe, USA, Canada, Australia, Japan

Cover: Foto ©ninafisch / pixelio.de

More available books at **www.hansebooks.com**

COMMODORE BAINBRIDGE

FROM THE GUNROOM TO THE QUARTER-DECK

BY

JAMES BARNES

AUTHOR OF MIDSHIPMAN FARRAGUT, FOR
KING OR COUNTRY, NAVAL ACTIONS OF
THE WAR OF 1812, A LOYAL TRAITOR, ETC.

ILLUSTRATED BY GEORGE GIBBS AND OTHERS

SCIMITAR PRESENTED TO COMMODORE
BAINBRIDGE BY THE MOHAMMED D'GHIES

NEW YORK

D. APPLETON AND COMPANY

1897

Copyright, 1897,
By D. APPLETON AND COMPANY.

PUBLISHER'S NOTE.

It will be of interest to know that the miniature portrait of Mrs. Bainbridge, the scimiter presented by Sidi Mohammed D'Ghiers, and the sword presented by General Hislop are all reproduced from the originals in the possession of a family descended from Commodore Bainbridge, which includes among its number the author of this book. This circumstance readily suggests the exceptional opportunities at the author's command in the way of unpublished letters and papers, and in a personal knowledge, which imparts a peculiar actuality to the scenes described in his story.

LIST OF FULL-PAGE ILLUSTRATIONS.

	FACING PAGE
The Java strikes	*Frontispiece*
Mutiny on the Cantor	16
On the deck of the Volontier	47
The Turkish admiral visits the Washington	76
The miniature of Mrs. Bainbridge	109
Decatur boarding the Philadelphia	130
Watching the bombardment from the Tripoli prison cell	138
Action between the Constitution and the Java	163
Bainbridge's reception at Boston	167

COMMODORE BAINBRIDGE.

CHAPTER I.

John Taylor, Esq., of Monmouth County, New Jersey, was walking slowly along beneath the shade of the trees bordering the path that led from the turnpike up to the big white house, an odd-looking building begun by his father and completed by himself, in an entirely different style of architecture, a score of years previous to the time this story begins. It had an air of ponderous prosperity.

As the old gentleman walked slowly up the path he took from his pocket a letter, the seal of which had already been broken, and thrusting his gold-headed stick beneath his arm, he re-read the epistle for the second time.

Mr. Taylor was stamped with the unmistakable air of wealth, respectability, and importance. One could see that his was a mind that came to conclusions slowly, and in the lines of his strongly marked old face a close student of character would have perceived firmness and resolution. He halted for an instant before he stepped out into the bright sunlight at the end of the row of trees, and finished his letter, reading the last words half aloud:

"I trust, my dear sir, that you will find our son tractable in disposition, willing and eager to meet your views, and obedient to your behests. Although he is so young, his mother and myself have discovered in him evidences of a lofty temperament, and I am sure that no lad could wish for a better promise for the future than the chance of spending his early life near one so able to teach the importance of high moral sentiments and proper rules of conduct as yourself. I shall bring William to you in the course of the next fortnight. Believe me, I am, most honored sir, your very devoted son-in-law, Absalom Bainbridge."

When Mr. Taylor reached the portico of the house he turned and looked back toward the big gateway and smiled broadly and pleasantly. It was almost as if he had seen some one whom he was glad to welcome walking toward him, and in his imagination the old man had pictured a boyish figure coming up the shaded walk.

Yes, it would be pleasing to have his grandson here; the old house had been lonely for many years. It would be a delightful task to again feel a young mind expanding under his control, for John Taylor was one of those natural-born instructors, a man with a gift of imparting information and controlling character.

As he stood there mopping his forehead with a large handkerchief, and smoothing back the thin, gray hair tied in a long queue down his back, his thoughts were interrupted by the approach of a little dried-up individual whose appearance showed that he occupied a position above that of a servant; but his manner was respectful, and was that of one well accustomed to Mr. Taylor's peculiarities. He coughed gently to attract the old gentleman's attention.

"Ah, Fenwick!" exclaimed the latter, turning. "Good news! My grandson is coming to us inside of a fortnight."

"I am very glad of that, sir," was the reply. "I was

much taken with the young gentleman at my first sight of him, sir."

With that the two old men entered the house.

Two weeks later a heavy, clumsy-looking coach rolled down the Middletown turnpike and stopped at the big gate of the Taylor place, and a boy of about thirteen years of age clambered down from the top. His box was handed to the roadside by the guard, and he stood there looking across the lawn at the great white house that seemed to smile a welcome from its wide-open doors and windows. There was no shade of sadness or despondency in the boy's face; he looked eagerly through the gateway as if expecting some one to come and meet him, and at this instant two figures appeared upon the veranda. His grandfather's appearance was well known to him, and although too far off to speak a word, he lifted his hat in a salutation at long range. Soon the old gentleman came hurrying down to meet him, accompanied by a servant, who shouldered the box and followed his master and the newcomer back to the house.

"Mother sends her love to you and my father sends assurances of his deep regard, and regrets that it was impossible for him, owing to his practice, sir, to accompany me," said the boy gravely, after the first words of greeting.

"And they are all well?" inquired Mr. Taylor kindly, but speaking as though he were addressing a man of mature age and understanding.

"All well, sir, I am glad to say."

"And so you wish to study to become a merchant, or mayhap a lawyer, eh, William?"

"I had rather be a sailor, sir."

"Highty-tighty!" exclaimed Mr. Taylor, lifting his eyebrows; "and what put such an idea as that into your head?"

"I thought about it a great deal, grandfather," the lad

answered. "In fact, ever since we came to New York I have liked to think of going to sea."

"What does your father say to it, William?"

"He says I'm too young to decide what I want; but I haven't spoken to him about it for a long time now."

"Then you would rather be a sailor and have to endure all the hardships of his precarious calling than to be a merchant and have dry ground under your feet, and a safe living always in peace and comfort?"

"Yes, sir, I think so."

"Well, well!" smiled the old man, a little nonplused at his grandson's calm frankness. "We'll see about all this after a while; perhaps you will change your mind."

"I think not, sir."

"We'll see," responded the grandfather. Then he went on to ask questions of the boy about his studies, his progress in the classics and languages, and to his delight he found him responsive and eager to learn.

Before the day was over John Taylor's heart went out to the son of his only daughter, and a great affection grew between them, to ripen into trust and confidence never to be displaced. And thus it is easy to perceive that young William Bainbridge's changing his home from that of his father, a hard-working physician in New York city, to the shelter of the mansion of his maternal grandfather augured well for his future career in life.

. . . . . .

Two very uneventful years followed in the peaceful New Jersey town. Studying with his grandfather and the village schoolmaster, young Bainbridge made great progress, and endeared himself to all those with whom he came in contact. But there is not space to tell of these early school days that flew by as quickly with William as they do with every boy. That unalterable inclination toward the life of a seafarer had led him upon more than one occasion respectfully to petition his parents and Mr. Taylor to grant him an opportunity of taking up early a profession in which sooner or later he believed he would find himself. He dreamed of ships and the sea.

Although Mr. Taylor had nothing to complain of in regard to the way he attended to his duties and pursued his studies, with great wisdom he saw at last that it would be best to grant the boy's request, and, instead of hindering him in fulfilling the wishes of his heart, he concluded, not without sorrow and some misgivings, to give him a good start, and place him in a position to make the best of any opportunities for advancement. To this end he wrote to Dr. Bainbridge a letter that surprised the good physician into an expression of astonishment, for it advocated placing William under the charge and patronage of a " respectable and intelligent commander " whom Grandfather Taylor knew was soon about to sail from Philadelphia.

" We had better let the lad follow his inclinations—a determined spirit may be broken, but not bent," read the letter. " Let him go to sea."

After some delay and much discussion, this was agreed to, and William, at the age of fifteen, started for Philadelphia with a letter in his pocket introducing him to Captain Waldron, well known as one of the most careful and painstaking officers then sailing out of the port of Philadelphia.

The good ship Ariel was his vessel, and, although she was small, she had made many voyages, and had the reputation of being a lucky ship with all the seamen—a point in her favor that offset her small size in securing a good crew.

Thus far this introductory chapter deals but slightly with the personal qualifications or the appearance of the hero of the succeeding tale, so before we follow him in his numerous adventures a few words are not amiss. He was a tall boy for his age, with a dignified, quiet manner, gentlemanly bearing, and a low, modulated voice. He was strong and active and of an adventurous disposition. In every boyish enterprise where peril was to be encountered, he had been the leader of his youthful comrades and many stories of his school days might be recounted. But we skip over the early life at Middletown to the very day on which began the career that has made his name famous among those "who go down to the sea in ships," and made him, moreover, a model for the young American sailor to look up to.

Fenwick, Mr. Taylor's confidential clerk and general major-domo, accompanied William on the way to Philadelphia. If there was one thing that the wizened little man objected to, it was the idea that any one in whom he felt an interest should display such a lack of appreciation as to choose to adopt the life of a seaman. And so William was compelled to listen to a long lecture, and many mournful predictions as to what might become of him after leaving good dry land.

He dreamed of the numerous dangers that Fenwick had called up to his mind—shipwreck and disaster, pirates and icebergs—but awoke the next morning undeterred and eager. He parted from his old friend at Burton's Coffee House after a hasty breakfast, and all alone he walked to the water front, to present himself to Captain Waldron on board the Ariel, then almost ready to set sail.

CHAPTER II.

"Well, my young gentleman," said Captain Waldron, looking up from a letter that he had just finished reading, "this is no time to make a speech to you; in fact we are so busy that I have hardly time for more than a few words, but those are words of welcome. We are glad to have you aboard. And I can promise you that you will have every opportunity given you to show what you are made of."

He surveyed young Bainbridge from head to foot, and then turning to one of the sailors, he directed him to take the little sea chest down below and show the young gentleman where he was to swing his hammock.

A great many captains in those days took out with them upon their voyages young boys who had shown a predilection for the sea, instructing them in seamanship and navigation, and thus many of the larger vessels were practically school-ships that turned out many young officers who afterward became famous in the service of their country, for, most unfortunately, the regular navy, during the ten years that followed the cessation of hostilities between Great Britain and the United States, had dwindled into nothing.

Captain Waldron's vessel was not large enough to accommodate many young gentlemen, and upon this voyage Bainbridge found himself the only scholar.

"That's a likely youngster," observed the captain to his first mate, his eyes following William's figure as it disappeared down the companion way. "I can tell by the looks of a lad how he's going to move. He's quick-handed and quick-witted, mark my words, Mr. Seth. There's a topman and an officer, too, in the make-up of him."

Mr. Seth was not altogether an optimistic person. He was curt and short-spoken in his manner, and a believer in the hard school from which he had graduated, for he had worked his way from the forecastle to the quarter-deck, and had not "come in through the cabin window," as he expressed it.

"Three weeks at sea will show us more about the lad," he observed. "But I confess, sir, I rather like the cut of his jib myself."

"I wish you to give him every opportunity, Mr. Seth."

"Be easy on that score, sir," Mr. Seth made answer. "He will not be neglected."

And this was a fact. Before the Ariel was four weeks from land young Bainbridge had proved, even to the first mate's satisfaction, that the choice of his calling had not been made haphazard. He could lay upon the yard with the best of them. His work was thoroughly done, and he kept his eyes and ears open to such good advantage that even before the return voyage was over he was no longer counted a green hand, and had lost all traits that mark the landsman.

Captain Waldron was delighted. Although not given to praising, upon one occasion, when Bainbridge had surprised him by his alertness and good judgment, he placed his hands on the boy's shoulder.

"My son," he said, "some youngsters I've advised to go home and seek a place in the counting house, some few to return to their mothers, but the sea is the place for you, there's no mistaking."

Thus when Bainbridge returned home from his maiden

voyage his family found him well launched in his career, and Grandfather Taylor did not regret the fact that he had been instrumental in helping to provide the merchant service with so proficient a candidate for honors.

For three years he sailed with his good friend Captain Waldron, and at the age of eighteen the latter wrote to the firm that owned the Ariel, stating that, if they wished to keep the services of young Bainbridge, they had better offer him a berth aft at the earliest possible moment, despite the fact of his extreme youth. The captain concluded by saying that he should have been glad to take him out with him as first officer on his next voyage, but, he added, he was reluctantly compelled to stay on shore for some months, and he bespoke for his young charge the first vacant position that could be found on any ship of the company that might be sailing.

William was paying a visit to the parents in New York when he received the notice of his appointment as first mate of the ship Cantor, sailing in the Holland trade. His stay on shore was cut short, and he hurried to Philadelphia to assume his post.

Before young Bainbridge had been on board of the Cantor half an hour he found that his position was to be very different from that of first mate on the vessel on which he had previously served. It needed but a glance at the crew to determine that the men were a bad lot, and the captain was not the man to have been placed in charge of them. He was undersized, and did not possess an air of authority.

It was the day previous to sailing, but the crew, at least those of them that were on board, were in various stages of intoxication. The cargo had been stowed, and Captain Stebbins was waiting for the tide, to set sail on the following morning.

Bainbridge looked older than his years. He stood

five feet eleven inches, and weighed about one hundred and eighty pounds. His broad shoulders and deep chest, and the tremendous strength of his arms and back, together with the fearless glance of his eye, gave him the appearance of being at least four or five years older than he really was. But he longed for Captain Waldron and Mr. Seth, and his fears that there might be trouble before long were verified by the first words spoken by Captain Stebbins after their greeting.

"Glad to see you, Mr. Bainbridge, and I might as well tell you that I am agreeably disappointed, sir. I had been told that you were but a lad who had secured this appointment through family influence. It will be a man's job to handle that lot of cutthroats—just look at them!"

Bainbridge glanced at the forecastle where three or four surly, hangdog-looking villains were sitting with their backs against the rail. Then he looked at Captain Stebbins's irresolute face, and again at the group on the forecastle. One of the men at this moment produced a big black bottle and, without any effort at concealment, passed it to his comrades. Each one of them took a pull, and the last half-insolently held the bottle up to the light and said in words loud enough to be heard well aft:

"Here's to the young gentleman on the quarter-deck."

"Hadn't you better stop that, sir?" inquired Bainbridge politely of the captain.

The latter turned his head away.

"I'm afraid to attempt it, Mr. Bainbridge, just now; 'twas hard enough to get a crew as it is. In fact, I had to pay them something in advance, and I fear me they would leave the ship—wait till we get to sea. We can't prevent it now."

"I think I can prevent it, sir," Bainbridge answered quietly, "if you will allow me to make the attempt. Are they all on board?"

"All but two. I suppose they'll come on board to-night drunk as the others."

It was indeed a bad lookout. But the young officer's temper had risen.

"I should like to make the attempt to put a stop to it, sir, if I may, during my watch."

"Very good; then it's your watch now," answered the captain, a little provoked and showing it plainly. "I shall be below."

"Will you tell me the names of the men as they sit there, sir?"

The captain answered, speaking in a whisper, giving the names of the men in order. The fellow who had proposed the insolent toast answered to the sobriquet of "Whisky Jack," but his real name was Monson.

No sooner had the captain disappeared than Bainbridge walked forward to the mast.

"Monson," he called, "step aft here, my man."

The sailor lurched unsteadily to his feet, and, followed by all of his companions (there were six of them), obeyed the order with a leer on his sodden countenance.

"The rest of you stay forward; I want to speak to this lad alone."

It was rather a strange thing for a boy of eighteen to address a man of at least forty in these terms, but there was no mistaking the import of his tone. A sailor knows quicker than any other man when he meets his master, and the rest halted waiting to see what Whisky Jack would do. Bainbridge did not speak a word. With his arms folded he looked the approaching man full in the face. The latter shuffled uneasily as he attempted to reply to the first mate's steady gaze. The leer faded from his face, and slowly his fingers rose to his forehead.

"Well, sir?" he said thickly.

"Fetch me that bottle."

"What bottle, sir?"

There was no reply for an instant. Bainbridge's face had a dangerous, set expression, but he repeated his order, if anything more quietly and calmly than before.

"Fetch me that bottle!"

The man turned and walked forward.

"The young gentleman wants a drink, Bill," he said, as if trying to keep up appearances. "Let's let him have it."

The fellow addressed as Bill grinned, and produced the bottle from his jacket, and Monson again walked up to his officer. Bainbridge extended his hand.

"Give it me," he said.

With a last attempt at bravado the sailor began to remove the cork.

"Never mind that," and with a quick movement the bottle was snatched from his grasp and tossed over the rail.

"Now, below, every man-jack of you!" thundered the first mate, stepping forward.

It was very wonderful indeed, almost past believing, in fact, but the discomfited group had no time to parley. Without a question they stumbled down the forward hatch.

The vessel yet lay moored alongside the wharf, and her rail was lower than the stringpiece.

"Well done, sir! This is Mr. Bainbridge, I presume," exclaimed some one, and looking up, William saw that an elderly man dressed in a rough sailor jacket was looking down at him.

"I'm Mr. Taft, second mate, sir," said the man, bending forward and climbing down to the vessel's deck. "That's the way to treat those drunken rascals. I'm glad to see it, sir, and I'd have begun it long ago myself if Captain Stebbins——"

"I was acting under Captain Stebbins's orders," interrupted Bainbridge, not wishing to discuss the actions of his commanding officer. "When will the rest of the crew be on board, Mr. Tait?"

"They're coming down the wharf now," the second officer made reply, "drunk as fiddlers."

And no sooner had he spoken than two more hard-featured individuals were seen climbing unsteadily down on to the forecastle.

"Monson," said Bainbridge, turning quickly to the sailor who had waited at the mainmast, "tell those men that I wish to speak to them."

With a look almost of admiration, Whisky Jack obeyed the order.

"See here, my bullies," he exclaimed in an undertone to the other two, "we are not going to have such an easy time of it after all. There's an *officer* on board this ship. He wants to speak to you. Don't give him any back talk; won't do for a minute."

The two sailors came aft.

"Monson," said Bainbridge, "search these men."

Two more bottles of whisky went overboard.

At this juncture Captain Stebbins came on deck. The first mate had given a glance at the weather vane that surmounted a flagstaff on top of one of the near-by buildings. He remembered a bit of seamanship that he had seen Captain Waldron successfully execute when lying at a wharf. A light breeze was blowing from just the right direction. It would require no warping for the Cantor to back out of her slip.

"Had we not better get out into the stream and anchor, sir?" Bainbridge asked, then perceiving for the first time that Stebbins was suffering from the same ailment that affected the crew. But his head was clear enough to grasp the idea that had entered Bainbridge's mind.

"Perhaps we had," he acquiesced.

The second mate sprang on the dock, and with the assistance of Monson cast off the moorings; the two sailors who were sober enough to have some of their wits still about them were sent aloft, and soon the mizzen topsail was laid against the mast, then with the assistance of the current the little ship gained sternway and fell off into the stream. Scarcely had the end of her flying jib boom cleared the pier head when those of the crew who were below in the forecastle came rushing up on deck.

But another surprise was in store for the first officer. Captain Stebbins, irritated that he should have appeared to have lost authority, burst into a torrent of profanity. The men came crowding down to the waist. One of them detached a belaying pin from the bitts. It looked like mutiny. Bainbridge stepped to the captain's side.

"I understood you to say this is my watch, sir," he said quietly.

Stebbins glanced at him, and without another word went down into the cabin.

One of the foremast hands had constituted himself spokesman. He was of that type so feared by officers of ships—a natural disturber, a born loafer and sea lawyer, breeder of trouble in the forecastle.

"We're not on the high seas yet, my Bucko," he said defiantly, "and we're not to sail until to-morrow morning. We have a right to go ashore."

"Can you swim?" asked Bainbridge quietly. "If so, overboard with you, and be quick about it. Come, now, are you ready?"

The man looked over the side. It was February; the river was yet filled with floating cakes of ice.

"Too cold, eh?" Bainbridge went on; "well, then, go forward. All hands get ready to drop starboard anchor."

Whisky Jack was among the first to obey, and in surly fashion the others followed suit. They had found out, as he had said, that there was "an officer on board," and no mistake.

The first mate was very tired the next morning at daybreak when the anchor was weighed, for he had not closed his eyes all night, and as soon as the vessel was under way he sought his berth and fell into a troubled slumber. He could see that all the seafaring he had done was but child's play to the experience that was probably before him. In these surmisings he was correct.

Bad weather was encountered during the first two weeks in the open sea, and so busy were the crew handling the vessel when on watch, and so wearied were they when below, that little time was found for grumbling. It had not taken William very long to perceive one reason at least why it had been so difficult for the Cantor to secure a better crew. The vessel was small, scarcely more than three hundred tons burden, and Captain Stebbins had received rather a bad name.

It was easy to see that he was not so much of a martinet or a driver as a "nagger"; although of rather a cowardly disposition, he was great on bluster, threats, and profanity, and when good weather was met with, instead of relaxing a little, owing to the hard time that had just been gone through with, he kept the men hard at it—first one thing and then another, and rating them severely on the slightest provocation. It almost appeared as if he did this to retrieve what he thought he might have lost by his timid behavior when in port.

But at last they reached the English Channel, and dropped anchor in the roadstead of Rotterdam. On the second day of their arrival more trouble occurred. They had passed the customs and were going to begin the unloading of the vessel when an affair took place that came near relieving the old ship of her rather obnoxious commander in a summary way.

How the men had obtained anything to drink Bainbridge never found out; probably from some of the small boats that were rowing about, for none of the crew had been permitted to go ashore, the captain having landed in a small boat he had hailed from the quarter-deck. He had returned to the ship late in the evening. Bainbridge had been below in his berth writing a letter in order to send it back by a vessel nearly ready to set sail, when suddenly there came from the deck above a sound of scuffling feet.

What possessed him to think of danger he did not know, but reaching up to the rack above his head he drew forth a brace of heavy pistols and hurried out. At the door of the cabin he ran into Monson, almost knocking him full length against the ladder, so great was his haste to gain the deck.

"What are you doing here, you rascal?" he cried, helping the man to his feet.

Whisky Jack was very drunk.

"Hurry, sir," he said thickly. "I ain't no talebearer, but there'll be dirty work up there in a minute."

A muffled cry for help reached the first mate's ears. In two bounds he was on deck. It was almost pitch dark, but there was light enough to see a confused struggle off to the port side against the rail, and in the rays from the anchor light he noticed Mr. Taft fighting furiously in the arms of two of the strongest members of the crew. One of them had wound his arms about the second mate's throat, and was almost throttling him, while the other was attempting to pinion his arms down to his sides. The old man was no match for them, and it would have been all up in another moment if it had not been for Bainbridge's opportune appearance. He grasped one of

Mutiny on the Cantor.

the heavy pistols by the barrel and brought the butt down upon the nearest sailor's head. At this same instant he caught the other by the back of his collar and gave him a twist that set him off his feet; the man tripped and disappeared backward down the hatchway. Bainbridge's eyes had become better accustomed to the darkness by this time, and he saw that another struggling group was centered about a prostrate figure on the deck.

"Don't use your knife, you fool," grunted some one thickly; "just heave him overboard."

The first mate's onslaught was so sudden and so unexpected that even he himself afterward marveled at the results of it. There were five men against one, for the second mate had not yet recovered himself sufficiently to render assistance. Two of the mutineers went down under two separate strokes of the heavy pistol. The men were too drunk to do much fighting, and even at the best, Bainbridge would have been equal to both of them; but as he turned from giving the last blow his foot slipped and he fell forward on one knee. At this instant he saw standing above him one of the men with an open sheath knife in his hand. Quickly he raised the other pistol and pulled the trigger; the powder only flashed in the pan, and the knife descended at him viciously. But the point struck one of the buttons of his coat, and, being deflected, entered the cloth and ripped it open the full length.

But help came from an unexpected quarter. Whisky Jack made his way on deck, and probably could not have explained why he had chosen the weapon that he had, but a heavy bucket can do a great deal of damage when swung by a strong arm, and the blow that Jack delivered upon the head of the would-be assassin put him out of the fight.

Mr. Tait had gathered himself together, and, armed with a belaying pin, laid one of the two remaining seamen on the deck with a blow that opened his head and nearly was the end of him. The last man, who was the soberest, cried for mercy.

Captain Stebbins managed to get to his feet. He had been frightfully mauled and was trembling so he could hardly stand; but the mutiny was over, and in five minutes the three ringleaders, who were the least hurt, were below in irons.

This was an end of the trouble for some time, but when the Cantor was ready for her return voyage Stebbins refused to sail and resigned command of her. Although exceedingly short-handed, Bainbridge agreed to bring her back to America, which he successfully accomplished, landing in Philadelphia in the latter part of June.

But although he said nothing, the story of his manly conduct and his display of nautical skill on the return voyage reached the ears of the owners of the ship, and in conversation with him before he left for a short visit to his family in New York, the senior partner offered him command of the vessel on her next voyage if he wished to accept the position.

When William returned home, he found that his younger brother Joseph had also decided to take up the sea as a vocation, and was then absent on his first cruise to South America.

CHAPTER III.

So we find Bainbridge a full-fledged commander at the early age of nineteen. At his suggestion, some alterations were made in the Cantor's rig that improved her sailing qualities in a great measure, and, odd to relate, when it came to shipping a crew, Monson was one of the first to make application; and when it came to sailing, it was evident that he had taken pains to turn up particularly clean and sober.

Three successful cruises were made without occurrences of much importance—one to Haarlem, one into the Mediterranean, and one south to Brazil. Upon his return from the last, Bainbridge spent some time ashore, and in the spring of 1796 he was offered the command of the ship Hope, a new vessel belonging to the same firm by which he had always been employed. And in June of this year we find him lying at anchor in the Garonne opposite Bordeaux.

His vessel was one of the neatest in the harbor; all the metal shone, the decks where white and clean, and the paint work bright and well touched off. He had been most happy in securing good crews to work with him, and he had found out that to make a sailor contented he must be well fed and kept busy.

His first officer was the same Mr. Seth whom he had sailed with in the Ariel, and his second was a young Yankee, named Beebe, but a few years older than himself, who hailed from Portsmouth, New Hampshire, an adventurous fellow and a good all-around sailorman.

There were a number of American ships in port at the time, and one fine day Bainbridge called away his gig and rowed off to a large ship half again the size of his own, the Lafayette, of Boston, whose captain, Richard Samuelson, was an old sailor of Revolutionary fame. He was giving a dinner to the officers of the American vessels on this particular afternoon, and the talk about the table was mainly upon one subject, an all-engrossing one to the Yankee mariner—the high-handed behavior of Great Britain on the seas! There was not one of them who did not have some tale to tell of having had his vessel stopped and good seamen taken from him by the display of superior force, to begin a life of slavery on board of one of the great floating fortresses of King George.

"What are we going to do, gentlemen, may I ask?" said one of the younger captains from the foot of the table. "Remonstrance is worse than useless. Our representatives at St. James's Court can accomplish nothing. We have no vessels of the regular navy to enforce respect. We are completely at the mercy of these sea robbers—confusion to them! And so far as I can see there is no ending to it."

"It is the solemn truth," put in another. "I've lost five men in the last two voyages, and would probably have lost two more if my little brig couldn't leg it pretty well, I can tell you. They took my third mate, a man who went to school with me in Roxbury. Sad news did I have to write to his wife, and he but just married."

"What would the English think," exclaimed the first speaker, "if a ship of any other nation dared trifle with their merchantmen in this fashion? There'd be a fine hullabaloo, wouldn't there?"

"Oh, just another war!" remarked Captain Samuelson. "I wish that we had a few fine live-oak frigates afloat with men like my old friends, John Paul Jones, Nicholson, Barry, and Biddle, to command them. But no, the Government expects us to look out for ourselves. Bainbridge here—what experience has he had with the John Bullies?"

"I've been most fortunate, sir," responded Bainbridge, who was by far the youngest of the five men seated in the cabin; "but I think that we have been rather too submissive, perhaps; though I say it who should not, I might feel inclined to make a show of resistance. We might even persuade the country at large that it is worth while to take up cudgels in defense of their citizens abroad, as well as to fight for their interests at home."

"Well said, Captain Bainbridge," put in Captain Steele, of the brig Bangor. "But the only trouble is that we would probably be blown out of the water for our pains. It is well to have a locker full of foreign flags at one's disposal, I find it, and to know a few words of foreign lingo."

Bainbridge said nothing, but he had long ago made up his mind to one thing: He would permit no one to search his vessel or to rob him without a show of the strongest remonstrance. He was afraid that if he spoke his full mind upon this occasion he might be regarded as blustering, a thing absolutely impossible to his nature, as he had never made a threat or a promise in his life that he did not intend at the time to carry out.

It had been his good fortune, as already stated, to have escaped the numerous discomfitures that had fallen to the lot of most of his companions at the dinner, but he knew that sooner or later their experience would be his. Proud of his country and jealous of the rights of her citizens, it rankled deeply to think that he would have to submit to the indignities of which he had heard the others tell.

But this day was not to go by without incident of more importance than a dinner party. As his gig neared the side of the Hope, that was lying quite a distance out in the harbor alongside of the vessel hailing from Charleston, South Carolina, he suddenly perceived a commotion on the deck of the latter—voices in loud talk, a sudden hoarse cry, and then a hail.

"Ho, on board the ship there! Help! Mutiny!"

Bainbridge had not left the deck, but at the cry he hastened below, and opening a chest, he drew out the two big pistols that had served him in such good stead on board the Cantor. He hastened up again and jumped into the gig. In three minutes he was alongside the other vessel, and followed by half his crew, he climbed on deck.

Without a shot being fired or blood spilled, the rioters were made prisoners and placed in irons. Then, after receiving the thanks of the captain, Bainbridge rowed back to the Hope.

As he was lifting the lid of the chest to stow the pistols away, the vessel lurched a little and the lid fell down upon his forearm, but unfortunately in such a way as to touch the hammer of one of the pistols, which was discharged, the flame igniting a bag of powder which lay in a compartment of the chest. Instantly there was an explosion, and Bainbridge was hurled across the cabin, badly wounded in his legs and the upper portion of his body. The crew, who were hoisting the gig out of the water, rushed down to see what had happened. A few buckets of water extinguished the flames, and a doctor came off shore at once. He pronounced Bainbridge dangerously hurt, but stated that he had a fair chance of recovery.

No one could have been nursed more carefully than he was by his officers and crew, each vying with the other to see what he could do for the injured commander. In five weeks he was able to be about the deck again, and in such a healthy condition was he that his wounds healed almost immediately. In a fortnight the Hope was loaded with a cargo, and weighed anchor for the island of St. Thomas.

The crew of the little ship was composed of a fine lot of sailormen. They were, without exception, full-blooded Yankees, although the cook was a black, and hailed from the island of Barbadoes.

Bainbridge had never had any trouble with them, and had always found them willing and eager. Very different indeed was his position from that he had held on board the Cantor when he had under him the crowd of half-drunken scalawags.

Just before the sailing of the Hope an American vessel had come into port and dropped anchor close to hand. She reported that ten days previously she had been boarded by an English cruiser, and no less than three of her crew had been taken from her by main force—deliberately kidnapped! Bainbridge's blood boiled when he heard the story, and a firm determination was formed in his mind to resist to the very last any attempt that the English might make to force such treatment upon him.

The second day at sea he called the crew to the waist and made a short speech—something he had never found occasion to do before.

"Men," he said quietly, "I do not intend to allow this vessel to be robbed, and I know that you will understand my meaning when I say that if any press officer boards us and takes one of you away he will have to take the rest of us also, and probably the ship into the bargain."

With that the Hope's crew were told off into divisions and a gun captain was appointed for each one of the four nine-pounders. They did not make a very formidable array, to confess the truth, as each gun captain found himself in command of exactly one man, for the number of souls on board the Hope was but eleven—eight seamen and three officers.

During the calm weather that followed for several days the men were worked at the guns. A target was towed out from the side of the ship, and good practice was made with the little broadsides.

No occasion was found for their immediate use, however, and Bainbridge's usual good fortune seemed to follow him; but late one afternoon, off the island of St. John, a small schooner was seen bearing down, carrying all sail and evidently intending to speak the Hope.

Bainbridge might have run for it and escaped, but the small size of the vessel made him think that he had nothing to fear from her, and he held his course. Before the schooner came within hailing distance he raised the American flag at his peak, and, calling all hands, had the nine-pounders loaded with as much powder as he thought they could possibly stand, and double-shotted, and for good measure a handful of musket balls was added to each charge. Loaded muskets, two to each man, were placed along the bulwarks, and everything was made handy in case resistance should become necessary, for there was no doubt that the schooner was one of the small English cruisers whose commanders took it upon themselves to stop American ships at every opportunity, and, trusting to the prestige of the royal service, insist upon the right of search.

Very soon the schooner had ranged alongside. She had not displayed her flag, but an officer in a cocked hat and a brilliant uniform was seen standing near the rail on the quarter-deck, trumpet in hand. Although the latter instrument was not needed, he placed it to his lip, and, disdaining the usual formalities, he bellowed at top voice:

"On board the ship there! Heave to! I'm going to send a boat off to you."

Bainbridge stepped to the side of the Hope. He saw that the little schooner carried four guns of a side, but they were of no heavier metal than his own, although, of course, they were twice the number.

The men had all come to the port side, and the nine-pounders had been cast loose. Everything was in readiness.

"I'm sorry I can't stop," Bainbridge shouted in answer to the Britisher's hail. "We are in a great hurry to-day."

"Perhaps they're in some distress, Captain Bainbridge," suggested Mr. Beebe.

"They may be in a minute," suggested one of the gun captains who had overheard the remark, slapping the breech of his gun with a chuckle.

"Heave to!" shouted the Englishman, disdaining to use his trumpet this time. "Heave to, or I'll fire a shot into you."

"I advise you not, sir," was Bainbridge's return to this.

The conversation had evidently caused some surprise to be felt on board the schooner, and, as the two vessels were now so close that everything could be observed clearly, it was noticed that the men employed in casting the lashings off the small quarter boat stopped their work; and that very deliberately the forward gun was run in and loaded. As the Hope was all prepared, her men stood apparently inactive along the bulwarks.

"Ready there!" said Bainbridge quietly; "if a shot touches us, let them have it."

Grimly he waited for the Englishman to take the initiative.

Bang! went the first gun. The ball plashed harmlessly across the bows.

"Steady!" ordered Bainbridge. "Don't fire until she hits us."

It was evident that the commander of the schooner

did not know what to make of the unexpected behavior of the Yankee vessel, for, instead of seeing her heave to with all evidences of consternation and fright, there she was sailing along as if nothing had occurred, with her commander looking over the rail with his arms folded, apparently unconcerned.

The Englishman's next order was heard by every one of the Hope's crew as well as by those for whose ears it was intended.

"Fire into her!" he roared.

Plainly he did not think it worth while to discharge his broadside, for the same gun was loaded, but this time with the intention of doing damage.

Bang! it went the second time. A long splinter whirred across the Hope's deck and the ball, deflecting, plunked through one side of the deck house and out the other, making a great crash among the "doctor's" pans and kettles. But before the John Bulls could see the result of their marksmanship the doubled-shotted guns of the Hope had answered. Away went the schooner's gaff and the main-topmast, brought down by the after gun, while the forward division of one, with equal good fortune, shot away the flying jib boom and the fore-topmast stay.

The shoe was on the other foot now! The man at the schooner's helm became confused, and Bainbridge had to come about to avoid collision; or perhaps it was the British captain's intention to board. So close did she cross the bows of the Hope that the latter's jib boom struck her side, carrying away all her starboard shrouds and braces. She fell off rapidly to leeward, and as she did so found time to discharge a gun of her port battery, the ball lodging in the Hope's mainmast.

But Bainbridge's starboard guns were double-shotted also, and the answer they gave to this was almost as disastrous to the schooner as the first reply had been. One ball entered near the fore chains, and another, coming through the port, dismounted one of the guns, killing or wounding three or four of the crew. The second gun had put two balls into the schooner's side, ripping a gash but a foot or so above the water line.

So great was the confusion on board of her that Bainbridge could see her crew running hither and thither as if they had lost their heads completely. But what was his surprise when he saw the English ensign run a short way up on the color halyards that flapped from the wounded peak, and then hauled down again.

"We've surrendered!" shrieked the English captain, who but a few minutes before had been so full of importance and bravado. "Cease firing, for Heaven's sake!"

Here was a pretty mess. Great Britain and the United States were ostensibly at peace. There was a strong party in the United States who deprecated any idea of resistance to the Crown, and what would be the consequences of his action Bainbridge could not foresee.

Paying no attention to the words he had just heard, he raised his voice and called an answer slowly back:

"What schooner is that?"

"Her Majesty's schooner Linnet, commanded by Captain Sir Philip Townes. What ship is that?"

Before Bainbridge could reply to this the action of his own crew drew his attention. They had given three cheers when they saw the English flag come down, and now, much excited, they were gathered in a body, evidently waiting for further orders.

"Shall we board and take possession of her, sir?" asked Mr. Beebe eagerly.

"Not for the world," replied Bainbridge. "Those guns were put on board of us for our defense, and we have used them for that purpose, but we have no right to put a foot on board that vessel. Our lives would pay the forfeit, and justly too, sir."

The crew looked a little disappointed, and some were quite angered that they should not be allowed to take advantage of their victory, but Bainbridge's course was the only one left open, for had he dared to treat the Linnet as a prize, he would have been guilty of piracy, or something akin to it. So seeing that the Englishman was yet waiting for an answer and displaying no indication of a desire either to escape or to renew the action, he called across the water to him:

"Schooner there! Will Captain Sir Philip Townes pray go about his business in peace, and report to his masters that if they want this ship they must send a greater force or a more skillful commander?"

With that he squared his yards and cleared away on the course for St. Thomas, leaving the English captain to chew the bitter end of reflection, to his own enlightenment it is to be hoped.

Although Bainbridge did not mention the affair except in a short report to the owners of the Hope, the news of it was soon traveling about Philadelphia within a few days of his arrival, and before he left to pay a visit to his friends in New York he had been offered the pick of the finest vessels then lying in the port of Philadelphia.

The English captain had thought fit to belittle the affair more than likely, or he had failed to make a report of it altogether. There was no complaint made to the United States Government, and it is doubtful whether Sir Philip's masters ever received the message sent to them.

CHAPTER IV.

When Bainbridge returned to Philadelphia after his visit to his parents he decided not to desert the owners of the Hope for a more ambitious command, but to make at least one more voyage in the little vessel before he turned her over to other hands. He knew her tricks and her manners, and he found that the large proportion of the crew were anxious to ship with him once again.

Mr. Seth had obtained a vessel of his own. Beebe was promoted to be first mate, and just previous to sailing, Bainbridge was fortunate enough to fill the latter's place with a young Philadelphian, Allen M'Kinsey, who, although he was but thirty-three years of age, had been eighteen years at sea, a tall water sailor and a good officer, although his lack of education had for a long time told against his securing a berth aft. His parents were respectable townsfolk; his father kept a small ship chandlery near the wharf.

The cargo was delivered successfully at Bordeaux, and after a short stay, Bainbridge by a most lucky chance was able to load his vessel with silks and wine and set sail, almost retracing his former course. Everything went well until within three hundred miles of the American coast, when at sunrise a large vessel was descried to windward drifting leisurely down upon the Hope before the light morning breeze. About nine o'clock she was near enough for it to be seen that she was a British line-of-battle ship, or better a razee—that is, a three-decker cut down to a ship of two decks only.

On she came, a fine sight to behold, with every stitch of canvas set, catching the gleams of the sun, the shadows shifting on her sails as she rolled lazily from side to side on the bosom of the long, easy swell.

When within speaking distance she hauled her wind a little, and without a hail dropped a boat cleverly from her quarter, and soon a young officer in a lieutenant's uniform hailed the little Yankee ship and requested " some one there on board " to heave a line to him. As no one apparently replied to that title, which was certainly as indefinite as it was insulting, the young officer scrambled on board over the low bulwarks, assisted by no one but the members of his crew.

Bainbridge was standing near the wheel with his hands folded in front of him, calmly waiting for the interview that he knew was soon forthcoming.

" Ship's this? " questioned the Englishman, straightening his cocked hat. " Is any one in command here? "

" I suppose you wish to inquire," responded Bainbridge, " the name of this vessel. It is the American ship Hope from Philadelphia, and if you are looking for the commanding officer, sir, you have the honor of addressing him."

" Very distinguished, I am sure. Have you your papers handy, my young Yankee? "

Bainbridge looked over the taffrail at the great shape of the battle ship, in whose shadow his own little vessel was then swallowed up completely. His brows knitted. It was odious that he had to stand and bear this insult, that he felt was more leveled at his country than at him, without doing anything to resist the imposition.

" Just wait a moment, please," he said politely. And going to the head of the companion ladder, he called the steward and told him to bring up the large tin box that stood in the corner of the cabin.

His leisurely movements angered the lieutenant, who exclaimed in irritation:

"Come, come, my man, make haste. You are squandering time."

"Not altogether," Bainbridge replied. "I am giving you a few minutes to think, so that you may act with care and discretion and regain your composure."

He looked the other squarely in the eye with his fearless glance as he spoke. And, as there was no reply made, he extended the papers to his unwelcome visitor, adding only:

"Read here for yourself. I have no one shipped with me who is not an American seaman; but I assure you, sir, that were it not for the fact that we are under the muzzles of yonder guns, you would not receive the satisfaction even of my assurance, or the pleasure of glancing over the paper that you now hold. There are my men; their appearance speaks for itself."

The boarding officer, who had been followed by five or six of the boat's crew, commenced to read the names in the order of their enlistment, but everything was so plainly as Bainbridge had stated it that it scarcely needed a glance to confirm his words. The men were passed and everything appeared to be over with, when suddenly the name of M'Kinsey caught the lieutenant's eye.

"This man here—M'Kinsey—where is he?" he asked as if with a ray of hope.

"He's my second officer," Bainbridge replied, "and is standing here beside me."

"You are a Scotchman," stated the officer positively, glancing from the paper in his hand to the face of the honest seaman.

"Any one who says that is a liar!" returned the young Philadelphian hotly.

"I'll make you eat that word," replied the Britisher.

stepping forward quickly. "Here, you two," he said, speaking to his own men, "lay hold of him and toss him into the boat. I'll break his heart for him."

Bainbridge quietly pushed his second mate to one side and, stepping between the two angry men, said quietly:

"Patience, sir, a moment; I know this man. He was born in Philadelphia. I know his parents. He is an American. I state this to you upon my honor. His reply to you was hasty, that I admit, but he had provocation."

"Provocation or no provocation," was the return, "he'll come with me, or I'll know the reason why."

"Just a moment," Bainbridge responded. "May I ask your name and that of your vessel?"

"I am Lieutenant Norton, of his Majesty's ship the Indefatigable, Sir Edward Pellew."

"Ah, so! Then does Lieutenant Norton mean to tell Captain Bainbridge that he lies?"

There was such a dangerous light in the young American's eyes that for an instant Lieutenant Norton hesitated.

"He may have deceived you," he half faltered. "He's Scotch."

"He has not deceived me. Do you intend to take him by force?"

"Do you intend to resist?"

"I am not so foolish; but I have no objections to *his* doing so.—Mr. M'Kinsey, in the corner of my cabin you will find two loaded pistols lying on the bunk. A sharpened cutlass hangs from the bulkhead close to hand. See if it is not as I say."

Suddenly turning, the mate jumped down the ladder, and as all this conversation had been heard by the crew grouped in the waist, an audible titter ran through the company.

"One's as good as another," the lieutenant growled,

trying to affect amusement to hide his discomfiture. "I'll take this man instead."

Reaching forward his hand, he seized one of the Hope's crew, a lad scarcely more than eighteen years of age but well-grown and hardy. Two of his henchmen caught the young fellow about the waist, and he was unceremoniously tossed over the side almost on the heads of those sitting below on the thwarts. But the officer did not wish to make his own exit with any degree of haste, although he perceived that there was a long pull ahead of him before he would again reach his ship, as she had edged off and now lay a couple of miles distant waiting for him. He turned to Bainbridge as if to make some parting sally, but the Yankee captain spoke first:

"Will you convey my compliments to your superior officer and congratulate him upon having so efficient a bailiff; and also inform him that for the young man you have robbed me of I shall take one of his Majesty's citizens serving in the first ship I meet, if her force does not preclude my attempting to do so. You know as well as I do that you have taken an American citizen to lead him into a life of slavery and bondage."

"You talk well," responded the lieutenant, "but no Yankee merchant captain would dare to impress one of his Majesty's subjects. A fig for your threatening, and good-day to you."

With that he dropped down into the boat and pulled away to the battle ship.

Five days afterward the lookout forward reported that there was a sail dead ahead holding the same course. Spreading all sail, Bainbridge made after her, and as the Hope proved to be much the faster he soon had the chase, a fine merchant brig, quite as large as his own little ship, under his lee. He raced down past her quarter, fired a shot across her bows, and suddenly hove short in front of her in such a way that the brig, in great consternation, let go all standing, and, with a tremendous fluttering and clattering of canvas, she swung about and heaved there up and down, helplessly confused. She was within easy hail, so Bainbridge called to her stating that he was going to board, and that if she attempted resistance he would blow her out of the water.

"Mr. Beebe,' he said, "board that brig; take nine men with you, and bring back a healthy John Bull— single and sober, and presumably industrious. Don't return without him."

If Mr. Beebe had not returned at all, he would have left the Hope in a very precarious condition, for there were then on board of her no one but the captain and second mate, and an old seaman on the forecastle!

When Beebe came on board the Englishman he saw to his consternation that she was much larger and more heavily armed than it was at first supposed, for she carried eight guns, and there were in the neighborhood of twenty seamen huddled on deck near the mainmast. For this reason he did not stop long to parley, but running up to a tall, tow-headed young fellow, he addressed the following question to him, roaring the words in his ear as he grasped him by the shoulder:

"Young man, are you married?"

"No, sir," faltered the seaman, taken all aback with the suddenness of the question.

"Then come with me," answered Beebe; and taking the sailor at a disadvantage, he grasped him from behind and hustled him across the deck through the gangway into the waiting boat before any one could lift a hand to prevent him. There was a rush made to the side, but the boat was almost an oar's length distant. In a few strokes Beebe had placed the prisoner, who was too frightened to resist, on board the Hope.

"Better get out of this," panted the first mate, running aft. "She's armed like a man-of-war, sir."

"Well, not before she takes a message that I have been longing to send, and wouldn't lose the chance of sending for the gain of a few minutes."

"On board the brig there! Will the captain make report that Captain William Bainbridge has taken one of his Majesty's subjects in retaliation for a seaman taken from the American ship Hope by Lieutenant Norton, of the Indefatigable razee, commanded by Sir Edward Pellew?"

Then sheeting home, the Hope was off before the brig managed "to get out of her own way," as M'Kinsey put it. Before night she was hull down, for she had not attempted a pursuit.

Bainbridge sent for the new hand.

"Young man," he said, "I am sorry for you; but now let's make the best of it. You'll be paid your wages from now on to the end of the cruise, and will be discharged at Philadelphia with money in your pocket, if"—and he paused—"if you do your duty. Otherwise your position may not be quite so comfortable. Step forward."

That was an end to it, although, of course, it did not make up for the hardships the poor lad had to undergo who was taken by Lieutenant Norton; but of this more hereafter.

The seaman was paid in full, and, as some one said at the time, he did not appear to be at all dissatisfied with either the service or the country into which he had been forced.

A writer of the early part of this century, in referring to this incident, said as follows: "The proceeding of Captain Bainbridge on this occasion was doubtless as illegal as the act which had provoked it; but to a mind like his, alive to the honor of his country and the rights of his fellow-citizens, especially of those under his immediate protection, the outrage he was compelled to witness by which a citizen of the United States was torn from his country and family, perhaps forever, was an apparent justification. Although it afforded no redress for the original wrong, yet it was designed to show the naval officers of Great Britain that the rights of American citizens, so far as they are committed to the protection of Captain Bainbridge, are not to be violated with impunity."

It was high time indeed that something should be done to settle the question of the assumed right of search that was to be brought to a conclusion some years later only by open hostilities between Great Britain and this country, in which Bainbridge was to have a proper arena for the display of his judgment, coolness, and good seamanship.

Once more he found himself much talked about, and accepted an offer made to him to take command of a large ship of some six hundred tons about to sail for the South.

After landing a cargo from New Orleans in an English port, he took another shipload for the West Indies. As part of his consignment was for the island of St. Bartholomew, a mere dot on the map, just north of the island of St. Christopher in the Caribbean Sea, he put into the harbor of Le Carénage, a commodious anchorage, but very difficult of access owing to the tortuous channel and abundant shoals. Just before he was ready to sail a period of calm weather began during which scarcely enough wind blew to lift a flag, let alone to waft a big vessel through a difficult passage.

CHAPTER V.

However, this unlooked-for calm, which under most circumstances would have proved annoying, turned out to be, as Bainbridge often asserted, the most fortunate happening of his life, and it involves a little romance well worth the telling.

St. Bartholomew was not the most delightful place in the world for a protracted stay, although the island is rich and fertile and produces large quantities of tobacco, cotton, and indigo; it contains no permanent springs, and it is impossible for a vessel fully to replenish her water supply there, as the inhabitants depend almost entirely upon the rainfall for drinking purposes.

At the time of which we are speaking there were scarcely more than twenty-five hundred white people and about eight thousand blacks on the island. The latter lived in huts scattered about the plantations, or in a little settlement of their own at the southern bend of the harbor, while the European colony was collected on the top of one of the sloping hills on the opposite side. The low white houses stood well back from the roads, surrounded by gardens of tropical luxuriance.

One day Bainbridge was walking up the palm-shaded walk with Monsieur Le Vidocq, a descendant of one of the earlier French settlers. He looked down upon the harbor, where his own vessel and one or two others were lying at anchor, and, turning, he spoke to the gentleman at his side, addressing him in French, for the young captain was quite as familiar with that language as he was with his own native tongue.

"Monsieur, I do not know what we will do if we do not get some wind very soon. Have you ever known a calm to last for so long a time?"

"Well, hardly, Captain Bainbridge," replied the Frenchman. "That is, not within my recollection. But probably in the course of the next few hours we will see a difference with the changing of the moon."

"Indeed, I hope so," Bainbridge replied, "or I may have to resort to kedging, a difficult process amid such tides and currents."

He turned again and looked at the still unruffled surface of the harbor, but just as he was about to resume his walk something arrested his attention, and he stood there without moving. It was the sound of a woman's voice singing to the accompaniment of a harp.

Monsieur Le Vidocq noticed the effect of the music upon his companion. "Ah, monsieur," he said, "you are listening to the voice of the Rose of St. Bartholomew, Miss Hyleger, the granddaughter of a distinguished Holland gentleman who has business interests here. Yes, it is most entrancing," he added, for Bainbridge had not moved.

"Indeed you are right, monsieur," he answered at last; "form and feature to accompany such a voice would be well-nigh perfection."

"And so it is," replied the other. "Monsieur le Capitaine, I have an idea. You must meet her and determine for yourself if, in my enthusiasm, I have overestimated the talents of this lovely person."

"Thank you indeed, my kind friend," Bainbridge replied so earnestly that the other could not but smile. "I accept your offer, and I pray you that, if it is your convenience, the meeting shall be soon."

He turned again to listen more to the low music when his eye happened to sweep out upon the harbor. A breeze had rippled the surface, and a little Swedish brig, lying far out, dropped all her sails as if to take advantage of it. For an instant duty drove all thoughts of the charmer from Bainbridge's mind. With a suddenness that existing circumstances were alone the excuse for, he apologized to the little Frenchman and ran hot foot down the hill to where his boat was waiting, drawn up in the sand. "Off to the ship!" he shouted to the three men at the oars; and in ten minutes the capstan falls were clicking merrily as the ship crawled up to her anchor. Then, as he had a moment to think, a disappointment came over him. He was not to meet the owner of that voice after all, and a deep regret seized upon him, which showed plainly what a strong impression the sweet notes had made upon his heart.

But the topsails had scarcely begun to draw when the breeze died away and the ship again lay entirely motionless upon the smooth surface. The little brig farther out held it but a little longer, and then dropped anchor with a hasty plash, as if angered at the failure of the elements to help her in her escape. But, although Bainbridge was anxious to leave the port, the dropping of his own "mud hook," as the sailor calls it, caused him no such feeling, and a boat rowed out to him early in the afternoon with the welcome tidings from Monsieur Le Vidocq that everything had been arranged, and that he would have an opportunity of meeting Mademoiselle Hyleger that evening at a dinner to be given to Captain Bainbridge at the kindly Frenchman's house.

When the young officer entered the large, low-ceilinged drawing-room, it took him but a glance to decide which one of the four ladies present was the possessor of the voice, for, seated on a divan in the corner of the room, was a tall, slender girl with a great mass of brown hair; her light-gray eyes looked up to him as the host introduced his guest, saying "the siren who so delightfully charmed us the other day."

"But Captain Bainbridge, unlike Ulysses, made no effort to escape," put in one of the other gentlemen who had listened to the introduction.

"When was it you heard me singing?" asked Miss Hyleger, roguishly glancing at Monsieur Le Vidocq.

"Yesterday morning, mademoiselle."

"Ah! then I can answer that the captain did do his best to escape, for shortly after practicing on the harp I walked out upon the veranda and was just in time to see him running down the hill. He put off in his boat and apparently did his very best to leave the harbor, in which he all but succeeded."

"The unfavoring winds were kindly," put in the captain at last, who, during this pleasantry, had been watching the play of Miss Hyleger's features and indulging in a strange fluttering of the heart hitherto unknown to him.

"A very paradoxical statement, sir," smiled the young lady, arising as she took his arm to go into the dining-room.

Well, the long and short of it was that Bainbridge did not leave the island that day, or the next, or the next. In fact it was quite a week before the wind blew sufficiently hard to carry him out past the headland and beyond the rocky reefs.

From the wide veranda of a low white house upon the hillside a tall young girl in a white dress stood half leaning against one of the portico pillars. Her eyes had a suspicion of tears, but she did not move from her position until she had seen the big ship break out into a cloud of swelling, gleaming sails as she reached the safe waters outside the shoals.

Captain Bainbridge, as he looked back at the hillside, realized that this little island, scarcely twenty-five square miles in extent, contained all in the world for him, and he once had imagined that he saw the flash of a signal as if a white kerchief was waved from the garden-shrouded porch of the house on the hilltop. He would return again, cargo or no cargo; to that he made up his mind; but he did not know how soon this event was going to occur. However, to his delight, when he reached his destination, one of the islands of the western archipelago, he found a letter from the owners instructing him to pick up a cargo of indigo and dyestuffs, and then set sail for Philadelphia.

Never was a ship unloaded so quickly, and almost one month to a day from the time he had left the harbor of Carénage his vessel, in charge of a native pilot, was a second time threading the narrow passage through the reefs.

A small boat left the little white jetty as soon as Bainbridge had come to anchor. Under the sturdy strokes of her black crew she was at the vessel's side almost before Bainbridge could complete his arrangement to receive his visitors, for he had noticed the little boat and knew who the two figures were that sat in the stern sheet; one was his friend the Frenchman, and the other was John Hyleger, who had been for many years Governor of St. Eustatius, one of the islands belonging to the Dutch Government.

Bainbridge was hard put to it to hide his eagerness when, after the greeting, he asked concerning the health of the Honorable John's granddaughter, who, although he did not know it, had been the first to sight the ship and had informed her grandfather and his friend of the American captain's approach.

In three weeks everything was ready for departure,

the wind blew strong and steady, the cargo was stowed, and the sails were loosened ready to be dropped at the word; but there was some delay. On shore at the little church, whose windows were wide open to the flower-scented breeze, a ceremony was going on, and when Captain Bainbridge, resplendent in a new blue coat with silver buttons as large as half dollars, rowed off to his ship, a woman's slender figure sat beside him in the stern sheets; she turned from a half-tearful gaze at the little island and two figures standing on the shore, to glance up into her husband's face, smiling bravely and confidently. Never was such a precious cargo carried by any ship that sailed under any flag for any port.

CHAPTER VI.

Mr. and Mrs. Bainbridge were exceedingly delighted when they met their new daughter, and a visit to John Taylor at Middletown resulted in the old gentleman's being completely captured by young Mrs. Bainbridge's tact and pleasant manners.

William Bainbridge was now in his twenty-fourth year. He had, as we have seen, assumed many responsibilities for so young a man, and had been through experiences and had surmounted difficulties in a way that would have done credit to any one many years his senior. But it was the old story of an old head on young shoulders, and people were apt to forget his youth after a few minutes' conversation with him, for his manners were grave and dignified, and his calm, unruffled temper never left him for a minute, no matter in what position he found himself. But his good spirits, his youth, and fearless nature were shown in the merry twinkle or the quick glance of his blue eye.

It was some time before Bainbridge went to sea again, and this came about from various reasons. The difficulties with France which led to the quasi war with that country had now opened a new field for enterprising and chivalrous exertion. The Government had found it necessary to organize a small navy for the protection of our commerce from the encroachments of the French privateers, and movements began at the various navy yards to rehabilitate the service, which had dwindled almost into nothing since the close of the war of the Revolution. There were not sufficient officers to man the projected vessels unless the merchant marine was appealed to, for there were few indeed who had received any instruction at all in regulation naval duties or manœuvres. Of course a few older officers who had distinguished themselves in the war of the Revolution could be still depended upon, but judicious selection from among the commanders of the American merchant vessels became necessary. Among the first names inscribed on the list of the Secretary of War, who was then acting as Secretary of the Navy, was that of William Bainbridge, already his reputation for decision of character and bravery was widespread, and when Captain Decatur (whose son, Stephen Decatur, was so soon to distinguish himself) brought into port the schooner L'Incroyable, just taken as a prize from the French by the sloop-of-war Delaware, the command of her was offered to Captain Bainbridge. In a few months the vessel was outfitted, and under a new name, the Retaliation, she set sail in September, 1789, in company with the brig Norfolk under the command of Captain Williams.

The two small vessels were under orders to cruise in Southern waters, where they were to join the flag of Commodore Murray, who commanded the frigate Montezuma. The islands of the West Indies were dangerous sailing grounds for peaceable and unarmed merchantmen. Pirates teemed in the Gulf, and the French privateers, who fell but little short of being freebooters, rendezvoused at various ports and preyed rather indiscriminately upon all vessels weaker than themselves.

It might be said that although no open declaration of war had taken place as an official act, yet France (then under a Republican form of government) and her sister republic, whom she had helped not long before, were at odds. Hostilities had commenced at sea, and overt acts were plenty.

But no adventure of any moment was met with until the first week of November, although one or two small French vessels had been chased into the protection of the harbors during the month of October. By this time the crew of the Retaliation had, owing to Bainbridge's untiring efforts, been changed from that of a merchant vessel to one having all the marks of a regular service. Strict discipline was maintained, and strong measures had been necessary to enforce it. But the officers knew their ship and knew their men, and the latter had begun to respect their commander. Commodore Murray had taken occasion to compliment him on the wonderful improvement accomplished under his direction.

Off the island of Guadeloupe at sunrise one bright morning during the first week of November, three sail were discovered bearing east-south-east and only about two leagues distant. At about the same time two other vessels hove in sight to the westward, upon which the commodore signaled Bainbridge to hold his course, while he in the Montezuma and Captain Williams in the Norfolk bore away in chase of the strangers to the west. It was thought that the three sails first sighted were British, so Bainbridge kept on his way and was not surprised when he saw the English colors go up to the peak of the leading frigate. Nearer they approached, but, when at about pistol-shot distance, down came the English flag and up went that of France. One of the big fellows fired a broadside that brought a few spars to deck and smashed into the bulwarks of the Retaliation, and at the same time another ranged alongside and ordered the commander of the schooner to lower his flag and repair on board immediately.

Bainbridge was totally unprepared for making any resistance, and as the ship on his port hand carried forty-four guns, and the one on the other carried thirty-six, there was nothing else to do but give in. Sadly he saw his flag come down, and calling away his boat, he rowed off to the larger vessel in obedience to the order. She was a fine craft, but at half a glance he could see that things existed on board of her that would not be tolerated on board an English or an American vessel of the regular service. The men appeared slovenly and the decks were littered about with various odds and ends, and untidy to a degree. As he walked up to the quarter-deck, a handsome, middle-aged man with a great deal of gold lace on the wide lapels of his long-tailed coat, approached him.

Bainbridge drew his sword and extended the hilt toward the resplendent stranger, balancing the blade across his forearm.

"May I ask to whom I have the honor of surrendering?"

"To Commodore St. Lawrence, of the navy of the French Republic. But as you had no opportunity to defend yourself, I beg you, sir, pray retain your sword."

Very politely he then asked the name of Bainbridge's vessel, and, learning of her former career, made some remark that might be translated into "turn about is fair play."

The Volontier, the flagship, remained hove to while she placed a prize crew on board the unfortunate Retaliation, but the other vessels, the larger of which Bainbridge learned was named L'Insurgent, accompanied by a little sloop, were making off after the Norfolk and the Montezuma, who had run out of their wind and whose chase had escaped them. Their capture appeared inevitable, and as the Volontier was a mile or so behind them, it appeared that she would be too late to take a hand in the action if there was to be one.

On the deck of the Volontier.

Bainbridge had joined the group of officers that had made their way forward to the forecastle, and with feelings of great distress he watched the two vessels ahead near the American ships, which had little chance of escape left them. Suddenly the French commodore turned to him.

"Monsieur," he said, "what is the size and armament of your two consorts yonder?"

Without hesitation Bainbridge made reply:

"The ship, sir, mounts twenty-eight long twelve-pounders and the brig twenty nine-pounders."

And if he breathed an inward prayer for thus doubling his friends' armaments, he must have smiled also to see the result of his *ruse de guerre*, for Commodore St. Lawrence, with a great deal of excitement in his manner and gestures, hustled his officers to right and left, loudly calling upon them to signal L'Insurgent and the smaller vessel to return.

Soon it was seen that the former had perceived her recall, for she came about and waited until the Volontier bore down within speaking distance. In the mean time the Norfolk and the Montezuma, having caught a new slant of wind, were making off, carrying all sail and growing smaller and smaller every minute of the time.

An amusing conversation now took place between the flagship and smaller frigate.

Captain Barro, the commander of the latter vessel, almost jumped up and down in his anger as he demanded the reason for his being called off just as he was about to capture both vessels; and upon the commodore stating that they were of "superior force," he went on to state, shrieking his words over the taffrail, for the two ships were now near together:

"I could have taken them both—both, monsieur. There was not a gun on board either heavier than a six-pounder." He hammered angrily upon the rail with his heavy cocked hat, almost weeping in his wrath and irritation.

The commodore, who had spoken hitherto in fairly good English, turned to Bainbridge, who was standing by, with difficulty repressing the smile that would rise to his lip.

"Did you not say, sir, that the force of these vessels was such as I have stated?"

"I did," responded Bainbridge sternly; "but if I could save two ships of my Government simply by misrepresenting their strength, I think I was justified in doing so. The circumstances warranted my hazarding the assertion, sir."

Perhaps St. Lawrence recognized the logic and made allowance for the temptation, for he said no more, and that evening requested Captain Bainbridge's presence at his table, as if nothing had occurred. During the course of his stay on board the Volontier he treated him with the greatest kindness and consideration, and presented him to General Desfourneaux, who was being sent out from France to Guadeloupe to supersede the famous Governor, Victor Hughes.

The day after the capture, the three vessels of war and their prize anchored in the harbor about six miles from Basse-Terre, the capital of the island, and the next morning all were landed.

The officers and crew of the Retaliation were ordered into close confinement in a loathsome prison; but, owing to the solicitation of his friend the commodore, Bainbridge and the commissioned officers were afterward brought off shore and allowed to remain on board the frigate, where they were given full liberty and treated with kindness.

On the tenth day Bainbridge was permitted to visit the shore on his parole of honor, for the purpose of arranging with General Desfourneaux, with whom he had had but a few words on shipboard, an exchange of prisoners, in accordance with instructions transmitted to him by Commodore Murray, who had sent a letter in to him by a Danish brig.

It was just at this time that the French people had begun that system of the affectation of extreme equality. Ceremony was dispensed with and a strange attitude of comradeship, simplicity, and make-believe frankness took its place.

Dressed in a quiet suit of citizen's clothing, Bainbridge awaited an audience with General Desfourneaux. In a few minutes he was admitted, and at once was asked to seat himself at table with *le general*, as the latter was about to take his luncheon. With the assertion that " sea fare did not agree with him," the general requested the young American to join him in the meal of a " blunt old soldier," and invited him to speak openly and frankly, as two citizens " would talk over their wine." The remarkable interview that followed is well worth a chapter to itself. But it did not take the young lieutenant (for that was but his actual rating in the service) long to determine that he was dealing with a wily old diplomat used to intrigue, and able to blow hot and cold with the same breath, despite his air of sincerity and *bonhomie*.

It would pay him well to be upon his guard.

CHAPTER VII.

" Now, captain," commenced the hoary old villain.

" Lieutenant, sir," put in Bainbridge, anxious to appear on even terms at the outset.

The general did not notice the interruption, except that he corrected himself in the next sentence, continuing:

" I do not wish you to consider yourself as a prisoner, lieutenant, or I do not desire that your comrades shall be treated as such. I pray you look upon your stopping here as if you were visitors detained merely from political motives. We intend to treat you as both friends and allies, I assure you."

In view of the fact that his crew were now lingering in a dungeon, this assertion appeared to be something remarkable, but it did not trouble the " blunt old soldier " in the slightest degree.

" Of course, it may seem strange, but I have long thought how great an advantage would accrue from the establishment of commercial relations between this beautiful island and your great country of the United States."

Bainbridge remained silent, waiting to hear what all this would lead up to, for he did not doubt that there was much more behind it.

" If you would but consider yourself the representative of your nation—which you are, for there are no others that rank you on the island—we could accomplish a great deal to the mutual advantage of countries," went on Desfourneaux, who had lost all interest in his soldier's fare. " I promise that I will liberate your men and officers, and restore your ship to you, if you will agree to consider, as the representative of your country, of course, the island of Guadeloupe as neutral during the *passage d'armes* between the French Republic and the United States."

Bainbridge saw the pit into which the other would draw him, and he replied calmly, after a moment's thought, choosing his words in order that he might not be misunderstood.

" You must know, general," he said, " that my authority extends no farther than to enter into an arrangement for an exchange of prisoners. If I took upon myself to enter into such negotiations as you mention, and they were disclaimed, you would place the United States in the position of an aggressor, which probably would please you. And whatever may be your views in regard to the condition of my men—I speak not for myself—I consider the crew of the Retaliation as not only being held in captivity, but as being treated with great barbarity."

The general then adopted a confidential tone in his reply: " I admit that it appears so, yes," he said; " but you see Monsieur Hughes has not yet left the island. I can not revoke his orders until his departure. This, allow me to say, is the explanation."

"General Desjourneaux," returned Bainbridge, " while your proposition seems very liberal, I can not see my way clear to assume this responsibility; but if you wish to make a cartel of my vessel, I will vouch that my country will exchange prisoners, man for man."

" I intend to include," put in the wily Governor, as if offering special inducements, " all of the political hostages now on the island."

Bainbridge, however, was not to be entrapped, and the curious interview was terminated without the Frenchman securing the upper hand. The " political hostages " were confined in a dungeon much too small for them. They were almost naked and in a state of starvation. Many of them were masters of vessels, and the jailer had proved himself to be a drunken, unfeeling brute. The news had been circulated among them that they were about to secure their liberty, and great rejoicing was the result; but they were doomed to sore disappointment. Their condition grew worse and worse, as if the new Governor had determined to wreak vengeance upon them.

Bainbridge had received assurances from Desfourneaux that they would be placed in better prisons, and at least treated as if they were human beings, but these promises came to naught, and the young officer found himself powerless to assist his unfortunate countrymen, although he boldly remonstrated against conduct so averse to the modern usages of war. Nothing but the fact that he had gained some powerful friends through his own personality prevented the Governor from placing him in close confinement.

About the last of December the Ponsea, frigate, from Point Petre, arrived at Guadeloupe, and on board of her were twenty or thirty Americans who had been captured by French privateers. In consequence of the diminution of the French force, as alleged by the captain of the frigate, these men had been compelled to do duty as part of the crew. Hearing of this occurrence, Bainbridge waited upon Desfourneaux, and alleged that as these men were prisoners of war they should not be kept in confinement where they might be compelled at any time to take up arms against their countrymen. He added that if they were neutrals, as the Governor had intimated in a previous conversation, there could be no excuse for their detention on board a public ship.

The Governor gave prompt assurance that the prisoners would be landed, as the vessel, he acknowledged, was within his jurisdiction. But the next day Bainbridge, to his anger and indignation, saw the Ponsea sailing for France without one of the Americans being released from their bondage. Angry at being thus trifled with, he again sought an interview, and a heated discussion followed, which ended in the Governor's renewing his offer to liberate all citizens of the United States, provided that Bainbridge would assume the responsibility he had hitherto refused. He also insisted that Bainbridge should use his best influence to open trade with Guadeloupe, although he knew what a nest of pirates the harbor was.

An extract from Bainbridge's letter, which he wrote a few days later, is of interest:

" *To His Excellency, the Governor of Guadeloupe.*

"SIR: As you are well aware that the prisons of Basse-Terre are crowded with my fellow-citizens, many of whom have been brought into port since my arrival, and as I know from my own observation that American merchant vessels have been here condemned as lawful prizes, your Excellency will excuse me if I express doubt of your good will toward either the Government or the citizens of the United States. You offer to restore the Retaliation to my command. I can not accept unless I am permitted to follow the instructions of my Government, viz., to capture all armed vessels sailing under the flag of the French Republic. The Retaliation is now a French prize, being captured by two of your national frigates. I can not take command of a vessel belonging to an enemy and give a pledge to be governed by an enemy's orders without disgracing myself as an officer and rendering myself liable to deserved punishment by a court martial. If I return in the Retaliation, she must be a cartel and commanded by a French officer.

"I have the honor to be yours, etc.,

"W. BAINBRIDGE."

The Governor was thrown into a frightful rage at this refusal to accept his proposition. He sent for the lieutenant and informed him of his intention to place him in close imprisonment, to which Bainbridge replied that no fear of punishment could induce him to abandon the principles which would always govern him as an officer of the American navy.

At last, wishing to conciliate the United States, even if he could obtain no pledge in advance, Desfourneaux fitted out a cartel, under the command of a French captain, and sent her with the Retaliation to the United States, the returned prisoners amounting to nearly three hundred.

In a final interview with Bainbridge he declared that he had resolved to compel the immediate departure of the Retaliation, and in the event of any act of hostility being committed previous to her arrival in the United States, he would put to death every American prisoner who might be hereafter captured or brought to the island. The cartel bore prepared dispatches to the President of the United States, in which General Desfourneaux made assurances of the neutral position of the island, and pointed to his release of the prisoners as a pledge of his sincerity. What he really feared was a blockade of his ports!

Bainbridge's conduct was highly approved of by the Government upon investigation, and he was immediately promoted to the rank of master and commander, and ordered to take charge of the brig-of-war Norfolk (the vessel he had saved), then lying in the Delaware River. He was given directions to fit her for active service as quickly as possible.

As soon as the brig was ready to proceed to sea, her commander was ordered to report to Commodore Truxton, then sailing with the frigate Constellation in the West Indies. He cruised among the Windward Islands, and took under his charge successfully several convoys of American merchantmen, among which was one fleet of one hundred and nineteen sail, bound to different ports of the United States.

Returning from this arduous service to New York in the month of August, Bainbridge learned to his great mortification that while absent there had been five lieutenants promoted over him to the rank of captain. He remonstrated in vain against this act of injustice, but received no reparation, except an assurance that it would not occur again. Nothing but his pride and attachment to the service, and the earnest solicitation of his friends, prevented his pursuing a course which would have deprived the navy of an efficient and capable officer.

Again he set sail on a cruise to the West Indies, where he captured a number of piratical craft, and landed on the island of Hispaniola, and on the 8th of November, off Cape Nicola Mole, he took the French armed vessel Republican and a prize that she had just taken.

On the 14th of November the young commander found himself at the head of a small squadron consisting of his own vessel the Norfolk, the brig Warren, and the sloop Pinckney, each carrying eighteen guns. With this small force he blockaded the harbor of Havana to prevent the escape of a large French privateer, and he did this so effectually that the latter vessel was dismantled, and ample protection was afforded to American merchant vessels cruising in Cuban waters.

Up to the time of Bainbridge's assuming command of

this station the French cruisers had preyed on the commerce of the United States to a vast and ruinous extent. But so untiring was his vigilance and exertion that for six months, during the most inclement and boisterous season of the year, his little squadron kept continually at sea, with the exception of ten days, when he was obliged to go into port for water and provisions.

The American merchants of Havana, upon his departure for the United States, presented him with the following letter, dated March 1, 1800:

"Having witnessed the ample protection which you have extended to American commerce trading to this island, it would be doing injustice to our feelings were we to suppress our acknowledgments of the vigilance, perseverance, and urbanity which have marked your conduct during your arduous command on this station.

"It must afford peculiar pleasure to the citizens of the United States to know that a trade which was so recently exposed to frequent depredations now passes in almost certain security; and we doubt not that they, with us, will do you the justice to acknowledge the essential services which you have rendered your country."

Sailing from Havana in March, Bainbridge arrived in Philadelphia early in April. He immediately proceeded home and found all his family well and anxiously awaiting him. To the delight of all his friends, and to his own satisfaction, he heard that his conduct had been viewed favorably by the President, and that he had been promoted to the rank of captain, his commission dating from the 1st of May, 1800. Only a few days later he was ordered to the command of the frigate George Washington, a fine vessel, and one of the largest in our navy. But his first orders were not calculated to give him much of either pride or pleasure in their execution; and this will be told about in the chapter that is to follow. It exposes truly a strange condition of affairs.

CHAPTER VIII.

John Taylor was seated in an armchair in the warm spring sunshine, and beside him sat the wife of his favorite grandson. Her head was leaning against the old gentleman's knee, and one of her hands was clasped in both of his.

"Indeed, my dear, it is hard to have him leave us again so soon; but I can tell you that it is an honor, of course, that he should accept the command of such a fine vessel; perhaps he may not be sent on the foreign service for some time, and we may have him here much longer with us. Hullo! who's coming up the road?" he added, breaking off suddenly and raising one hand to shade his eye.

"Some one on horseback," answered Mrs. Bainbridge, rising to her feet.

A man on a strong brown horse reined in at the steps and, leaping from the saddle, left the nag to nibble at the short spring turf.

"Dispatches for Captain Bainbridge, sir," he said, saluting.

"I'll bring them to him," said Mrs. Bainbridge, extending her hand. But she was saved the trouble, for just then the figure of Bainbridge himself appeared in the doorway. He took the package, and his handsome face clouded a little as he observed his wife's troubled look.

"Sailing orders, William?" she asked, her underlip trembling suspiciously.

"Yes, dear, I fear so."

Without breaking the seal he turned and went into the house. Mrs. Bainbridge again slipped her hand into old John Taylor's outstretched palm. A tear that she endeavored to hide stole down her cheek, but the old man had noticed it.

"A sailor's wife——" he began.

"Should be brave, I know," concluded his granddaughter, anticipating his remark; "but sometimes it does seem hard, I must confess."

A silence followed that was broken by the footsteps of Captain Bainbridge approaching down the hallway. It was evident that he was suffering from some irritation.

"Well, William," asked his grandfather, "what's the news? Welcome, I hope."

"Quite the reverse, sir," replied the captain. "I am ordered to take that infamous tribute to Algiers! A pretty commission for a gentleman and an officer to execute!"

"It is a disgrace to the country," exclaimed Grandfather Taylor, thumping down both fists on the arms of his chair.

"There is one kind of tribute I would like to give them," continued William, "and that is from the mouth of my guns. The idea that we, a Christian nation, and bound to be one of the most powerful, should permit such a scandal as buying immunity from a lot of Barbary pirates is almost as bad as submitting to the English right of search."

"If anything, it's worse," put in Mr. Taylor. "Think of the contempt that they must hold us in! 'Dogs of Christians' they call us."

"Well, there are others in the same position," Captain Bainbridge answered, sitting down on the lower step beside his wife. "Almost all of Europe pays tribute in one way or another."

"Except England," suggested Mr. Taylor.

"Ay, there's the rub!" was the answer. "It is my opinion that she supports these brigands and buccaneers in order to gain the supreme control of the commercial Mediterranean. Proof is not lacking to show that in this I am correct. They could suppress every pirate from Gibraltar to the Bosphorus in three months, but they would not have it otherwise than as it is."

In common with many of the officers and a large proportion of American citizens, Bainbridge held strong prejudices against Great Britain, and bewailed her influence. But, odd to relate, his grandfather, during the war of the Revolution, had been an opponent of rebellion, and his own father, Absalom Bainbridge, had been an out-and-out Tory and had moved to New York during the war in order that his children should be among the adherents of the Crown, who held the city. Nevertheless all of the younger generation had grown up stout patriots, and it had not taken the honest doctor very long to change his opinions, although he would never discuss the question under any provocation.

It is easy to see how a mission like the delivering of the tribute money to Algiers should gall so high-spirited a nature as was Bainbridge's; but duty was paramount, orders were to be obeyed, and as soon as the George Washington was in readiness and all arrangements had been completed he bade farewell to his wife and family and set sail.

He arrived at Algiers with the annual tribute, amounting to some twenty thousand dollars, which he placed in the hands of the United States consul, declining to assist in any ceremony of presentation to the Dey.

The George Washington was the strongest American frigate that the Algerines had ever seen, and in fact was one of the largest ships that ever dropped anchor in the harbor. She lay close in under the guns of two powerful batteries, and the wily Dey, a little angered, perhaps, at the short way in which the tribute had been paid to him, viewed the tall spars and finely modeled hull with envy

Algiers.

not unmingled with ire, and a brilliant idea entered his head. Why not humble this distant nation still more, and make use of the fine craft yonder as if it were his own? Acting upon this inspiration, he sent at once for the American consul, Mr. Richard O'Brien, a sagacious and intelligent man, who had been at a former period a prisoner in this very country.

After the audience with the regent, the consul left the palace and hastened to the shore, where he was fortunate enough to find a cutter of the George Washington waiting at the dock. Explaining to the cockswain the urgency of his desire to see Captain Bainbridge, he was placed on board at once.

Bainbridge received him in the cabin. Consul O'Brien was evidently in some distress of mind, so Bainbridge treated him cordially, asked him to sit down, at the same time dismissing a number of officers who were loitering at the table, for dinner was just over.

"Well, sir," he said, "what is amiss? What can I do for you?"

"I do not know what is to be done," responded the consul, "but I must speak quickly and to the point, even if I have to indulge in a short preamble. You know, Captain Bainbridge, that all the Barbary States are under the direct control and obey the commands of the Grand Seignior at Constantinople. They are practically hirelings and dependents upon the Turk and the Ottoman power. The present Dey—confound him!—has got himself into a mess with the Porte because he has concluded a treaty of peace with France just at this time when Turkey, and England, her ally, are carrying on the war in Egypt against the young General Bonaparte. There is the situation in a nutshell. Now it has entered his unscrupulous old head—bad luck to him!—that it would be a fine thing indeed to appease the heathen Turk by sending to him presents of money and various things that the old villain has stolen, and to have them accompanied by a special ambassador to Constantinople."

"Well, I can see no objection," returned Bainbridge.

"Yes; but, man dear—excuse me, Captain—he wants to send them in your ship—in the George Washington, that bears the flag of the United States, by all the powers!"

Bainbridge threw back his head and laughed heartily.

"Do you suppose for one minute that I intend to allow him to carry out his intentions?" he asked.

"But, my dear Captain, make note of this: he is a murdering old divil that will stop at nothing. Can't you sail out this very instant?"

"Not without some wind to sail with," responded Bainbridge, looking out of one of the after ports. "Can't you secure an audience for me with the regent? I should like to politely express my opinions to him."

"You will find that he is hard to change in his determinations," replied Mr. O'Brien. "Could you warp the vessel to the mouth of the harbor?"

"It would be a hard job," Bainbridge answered. "But for that matter, if they wanted to prevent my leaving, they could dismantle me before I had sailed a cable's length. Just look up there."

Over two hundred pieces of ordnance of heavy weight frowned down upon the frigate, and from innumerable loopholes in the castle a fire of musketry could have swept her decks and tops.

Near the entrance to the harbor two crescent-shaped batteries stood close to the water's edge, and at the inner bend of the anchorage another small fort looked out over the roadstead.

But the next morning Bainbridge found that Mr. O'Brien had been successful, and that the Dey would grant him an audience soon after his morning meal, which took place at noonday.

The captain found the Algerine potentate sitting cross-legged on a luxurious divan, being fanned by two large slaves, while his ministers sat at some distance about the walls. No chairs were provided, and during the interview, that was carried on by the aid of an interpreter, Bainbridge stood, and he stood very erect too, with folded arms, and indulged in none of the genuflections that characterize court etiquette in Algeria.

"Has the consul expressed my desires to the American captain?" was the first question the Dey asked.

"He has, and the American captain regrets that he can not comply with the distinguished request, as it would be contrary to the orders of his Government received before leaving home."

"That is all right on the other side of the water," the Dey responded, "but here my wishes are of more importance."

"That I deny," returned Bainbridge through the interpreter.

The Dey did not allow it to be seen how these words nettled him, but the retort that he made showed the position he intended to take in the matter.

"For what your country says," he sneered, "I care no more than for a handful of dried dates. You are in my power. It makes no matter to me whether you declare war or not. It would only make me richer and more powerful; but this much must be understood: either you take my ambassador and my presents to Constantinople or you sink where you are. And in three weeks my harbor shall be filled with American shipping. I have said."

At this moment O'Brien spoke up. He endeavored to explain the position in which Captain Bainbridge was placed. He informed the Dey that such procedure was contrary to all national law, and he said that the whole of Europe would revolt at such an arbitrary mode of procedure. But nothing moved the obstinate old Mussulman, and when Mr. O'Brien had finished speaking he intimated that the audience was at an end.

Once out in the open air, O'Brien expressed his feelings in no measured terms. Bainbridge was too angry to speak, but he was going over everything calmly and dispassionately in his mind. He knew that the Dey would make good his threats, and he thought of the unprotected commerce that would be at the mercy of the ruthless barbarian if the Algerines were turned loose to seek their prey.

"It is a good deal like having a man put a pistol to your head and order you to dance," remarked the consul.

"Yes, somewhat similar," Bainbridge returned. "What would you do in such a case?"

"By the saints, I suppose I'd foot it," answered the little Irish-American with a shrug of his shoulders. "Couldn't you slip your cable and get out under cover of darkness? I'd rather have a cargo of monkeys than a shipload of those heathen Turks for companions."

Bainbridge called a council of his officers that night in the cabin. It was impossible to slip out of the harbor, and the next morning he wrote the following letter, which he placed on board a small vessel bound for Spain, with instructions to put it on board the first home-bound American ship that might be met with. The epistle was addressed to the home Government, and, after the introductory form, it read as follows:

"The Dey of Algiers, soon after my arrival, made a demand that the United States ship George Washington should carry an ambassador to Constantinople, with presents to the amount of five or six hundred thousand dollars, and upward of two hundred Turkish passengers. Every effort was made by me to evade this demand, but it availed nothing. The light in which the chief of this regency looks upon the people of the United States may be inferred from his style of expression. He remarked to me: 'You pay me tribute, by which you become my slaves; I have therefore a right to order you as I may think proper.'

"The unpleasant situation in which I am placed must convince you that I have no alternative left but compliance, or a renewal of hostilities against our commerce. The loss of the frigate and the fear of slavery for myself and crew were the least circumstance to be apprehended; but I knew our valuable commerce in these seas would fall a sacrifice to the corsairs of this power, as we have here no cruisers to protect it. Inclosed is the correspondence between Richard O'Brien, consul general, and myself on the subject of the embassy, by which you will see that I had no choice in acting, but was governed by the tyrant in whose power I had fallen.

"I hope I may never again be sent to Algiers with tribute, unless I am authorized to deliver it from the mouth of our cannon. I trust that my conduct will be approved of by the President, for, with every desire to act rightly, it has caused me many unpleasant moments."

A strange assortment of presents they were, and only such as one barbaric power could send to another, and especially if that power had at some time had free access to the contents of various vessels of all nations. Silks and satins from French looms, cloth and handsome embroideries, plate and chinaware from various places, three handsome Arabian steeds, and two tame lion cubs were stored on board, and the retinue of the ambassador, numbering some two hundred Mohammedans, thronged the decks.

Bainbridge, having been forced to submit to this indignity, made up his mind to do it as gracefully as he could; but a crowning affront was to be offered him before he cleared the mouth of the harbor. An Algerine rowboat, manned by twenty oarsmen, came alongside the vessel with orders from the Dey that the George Washington should proceed to Constantinople flying the flag of Algiers! One was handed up to him for the purpose. Bainbridge called away his gig at once and, thoroughly angry, rowed ashore, and made his way to the palace. The Dey would not see him, but he carried on a conversation with him through one of his head men.

The American captain remonstrated in vain, and was forced at last to row back to the ship and hoist the hated flag at his peak while he flew the Stars and Stripes at his main and fore. Once outside of the harbor and beyond range of the guns that the Dey could bring to bear upon him, down came the green and yellow rag. The flag of the United States arose in its place, and, in some way that has never been accounted for, the Algerine emblem was lost overboard.

It was the nineteenth day of October in the year 1800 when the George Washington set sail from Algiers. Head winds and bad weather were encountered from the outset, and the crowded condition of the ship made every one uncomfortable.

The Mussulman is compelled by his religion to pray frequently at various stated intervals during the day, and a *sine qua non* is that he should face toward Mecca—in this instance toward the east. It was a remarkable sight to see the ambassador and his suite prostrating themselves upon the deck, and then, as the ship swung off upon another tack, rushing to the binnacle to be sure that their prayers were directed properly. With the sailors hauling and bawling about them, and not any too careful how they stepped among the worshiping Turks, it must have been a remarkable sight. In fact, it was very hard to manage the Algerines without resorting to severe measures, which would have been hardly proper under the circumstances, as they were supposed to be distinguished guests.

After fifty-nine days of severe tossing, the entrance to the Dardanelles was sighted, with the two large forts guarding the highway to Constantinople. Bainbridge took on board a pilot when some distance from the en-

trance, and as they approached the narrow gateway the
officer of the deck was told that it was always necessary
for foreign ships to come to anchor under the guns of the
great fortress to the east and await there the permission or firman from the Grand Seignior. Immediately
Bainbridge was informed, and the prospect of having to

The Dardanelles.

remain detained any longer than was absolutely necessary was most distressing to him. So stratagem was
determined upon to enable the George Washington to
overcome this obstacle.

The guns of the forward battery were loaded with a
double saluting charge, and the frigate, under the favoring wind, swept up the narrow channel, clewing up her
topsails and hauling down the jib as if it was her intention to anchor. It was a warm, hazy day; the ramparts
of the fort were seen to be lined with soldiers watching
the frigate as she approached. When about midway in
the passage, Bainbridge began to fire a salute of twenty-one guns, which he did as rapidly as they could be loaded
and primed. At once both forts began to answer. The

air clouded up with the white, opaque smoke, and when it cleared away the Turks must have been astonished to perceive the vessel they supposed they would find anchored near to them a full mile or more up the straits, bowling along with studding sails and royals set and drawing.

In the course of a few hours the George Washington dropped her anchor in the harbor of Constantinople, the first vessel in the history of man to have reached that place without first securing the permission of the Sultan. The frigate lay in the lower part of the harbor. It was the 9th of November, and late in the afternoon. The many minarets and slender spires and domes of the city gleamed in the sun. The gray castle and the fortifications that lined the water's edge were crowded, as the forts had been below, with troops of curious soldiery and citizens. Presently from the castle a boat put out, the rowers of which pulled long oars whose handles were weighted at the end, and they made her dance through the water at a lively pace.

A man with a large turban on his head sat in the stern sheets, and seeing that it was his intention to board, the ladder was hastily dropped, and in another instant he stood at the gangway.

"What vessel is this?" he asked, speaking very good French.

"The George Washington from the United States," Bainbridge replied, lifting his hat.

To every one's surprise, this answer was sufficient, for, without coming down upon the deck, the visitor hastened down to the boat, and at the same racing pace rowed back to the castle.

Before the sailors had finished rigging the starboard gangway he had again returned, and having boarded, he approached Captain Bainbridge and made a low obeisance.

"The Turkish Government sends greetings," he said. "But no one has ever heard here of such a Government as the United States. Will the captain please explicitly describe what country he hails from and what government he represents."

Bainbridge thought for a minute, and then made answer.

"Will you say to those who sent you," he said, discovering that the gayly caparisoned visitor was merely a messenger, "that this frigate comes from the country to the westward—the New World—discovered by Columbus?"

This seemed entirely satisfactory, and the turbaned one took his departure for the second time. In a few hours a larger boat was seen approaching with the same messenger, accompanied by an elderly man, and they came on board at once. They brought a lamb and a bunch of flowers, the former as an emblem of peace and the latter of welcome.

The elderly man proved to be the captain of the port, and he bore instructions to conduct the frigate into the inner harbor. The anchor was tripped as she entered into the mole, passing close to the castle and firing a salute of twenty-one guns, which apparently afforded much satisfaction and was returned promptly.

Half an hour after the George Washington had come to anchor, although it was now quite late, a boat rowed off to the ship with an invitation from the Grand Seignior for the American commander to appear before his august presence. The Algerine ambassador was not mentioned, although word had been sent of his arrival.

The Grand Seignior's first remark was upon the flag that he had particularly noticed.

"It is, like my own," he said, "decorated with one of the heavenly bodies, and I consider this coincidence a good omen of the future friendly intercourse between our respective nations. It is most probable that we have many affinities of laws, religion, and manners."

Bainbridge tried to explain in a few words a little about his country, and the Sultan displayed great interest but great ignorance. The next morning the Algerine ambassador reported himself at the palace but was denied an audience, word being sent to him to wait until the return of the Capudan Pasha, or High Admiral, then absent on a cruise. As the ambassador refused to leave the ship, Bainbridge was compelled to put up with him as a guest for some time longer; but he hoped the Capudan Pasha would not delay long, for he was anxious to get rid of his mission and proceed homeward.

The eighth day after the arrival of the George Washington a very resplendent dragoman came offshore, and by means of an interpreter, who spoke French, he inquired of Captain Bainbridge if the latter did not know that there was such an officer as the Reis Effendi in the city of Constantinople.

"You have reached this port," added the dragoman, "without either the consent or the acknowledgement of the Turkish Government—something without precedent —and you have neglected to report yourself to the proper officer, and thereby you have offered him an indignity which requires a reparation. His Supreme Royal Highness, the Reis Effendi, hereby orders you to report and appear before him to-morrow morning at ten o'clock."

Bainbridge was nonplused at first, but he concluded that it would be best to put on a bold front, although he did not know against whom he had offended.

"Although I command this ship, tell your master," he said, "I carry an ambassador with presents to the Sultan, and I feel under no obligations to hold intercourse with members of the Government other than an interchange of civilities."

"No matter what your own personal feelings may be," responded the dragoman, nodding significantly, "I advise you not to disobey the commands which I have delivered."

"I do not regard them as commands," Bainbridge said rather hotly, for the understrapper's insolence was calculated to disturb one's peace of mind. "And as for his threats, tell him they amount to nothing. This is all I have to say."

Upon thinking matters over later in the day, it seemed to him that it would be prudent to find out from some of the resident ministers of one of the countries friendly to the United States exactly what position the Effendi held, and what it would be best for him to do under the circumstances. As the United States had no representative at all at the Sultan's court, Bainbridge accordingly waited on Lord Elgin, the British ambassador, and told him the whole story, informing him of the message he had received from the Reis Effendi, and expressing a hope that the amicable relations then existing between their respective governments would justify his calling upon him for such aid as he might find necessary in case any trouble should arise.

Lord Elgin responded promptly by offering his friendly services, and stating that the object of the Reis Effendi was merely to obtain a bribe. He promised to send a message by his dragoman to the importunate gentleman that would prevent all further annoyance.

"You see, Captain Bainbridge," Lord Elgin said, "the Grand Vizier, or Reis Effendi, as he calls himself, is actually next in rank to the Sultan. But he and the latter are comparative strangers for the simple reason that the Ottoman potentate has no private correspondence or interviews with any high official of his Government unless it happens that the officer has some near relationship through blood or marriage—a most singular regulation, but in this case one that works to your favor, for the Effendi and the Sultan scarcely speak to one another, and only meet at public functions."

After expressions of gratitude for his lordship's kindness, Bainbridge put back to his ship, much reassured, for he was placed in a worse position in Constantinople than he was in the harbor of Algiers, having no one at all to represent his Government, and being under the guns of the fort, escape was beyond question.

Two weeks went by, and on the fourteenth day a man working up aloft shouted down to the deck of the George Washington that a large fleet of thirty or forty sail was approaching, distant about six or eight miles. Before sunset the Capudan Pasha, the Lord High Admiral, sailed in, just home from Egypt, with fifteen sail of the line and thirty smaller vessels. As the leading battle ship entered the harbor the George Washington fired a salute. But no answer was given, for at that moment a heavy squall blew across the Bosporus, and many of the vessels were taken all aback, the largest, the flagship, only being saved from going ashore by dexterous handling. Bainbridge was disappointed and hurt that no attention had been paid to his twenty-one guns. But the next morning, very early, he was informed that the admiral's private secretary, Mr. Zacbe, was waiting to see him. Upon being ushered into the captain's presence he advanced, and, omitting the low obeisance of the Ottoman, he extended his hand in European fashion, at the same time saying in good English:

"The admiral's compliments to Captain Bainbridge, and he regrets that an accident alone prevented his replying to the captain's courteous salute. He desires me to state that he will return it at noon to-day, gun for gun."

Bainbridge could not help expressing his delight at meeting one who was close to those high in authority, who could speak his language, and who knew about his country.

"Ah, indeed, I know of it well," returned the admiral's secretary. "I was educated in Paris and London, and while in the former place I had the great pleasure of meeting the illustrious Benjamin Franklin. Indeed, although I was a very young man, I might say that we became good friends."

Bainbridge was much taken with Mr. Zacbe's engaging manner, his demeanor, and intelligence, and he held quite a long conversation, in which the secretary expressed himself as a great admirer of the structure of our institutions, and displayed no little knowledge of our history. A friendship was thus commenced that lasted through many years; until Mr. Zacbe's death, in fact, regular correspondence was exchanged, although Bainbridge and he were so many thousands of miles apart.

Promptly at twelve o'clock the Turkish flagship fired a salute with broadside guns, after which the captain received an invitation to visit the admiral at his palace, which was near to that of the Sultan and not far from the water. Capudan Pasha received the American officer with the greatest hospitality and many protestations of delight.

CHAPTER IX.

When Lord Elgin was informed by Bainbridge that the Capudan Pasha had taken the George Washington under his immediate protection, he was profuse in his congratulations, stating that it was an honor that had been extended to few vessels, and was full of promise for any negotiations that he might seek to bring about, or any favors he might desire to ask.

"Your way is now paved," he said, "and no better opportunity could present itself for extending an *entente cordiale* between the Ottoman Government and your own."

Bainbridge saw this, and after his reception by the Turkish admiral he invited the latter on board the frigate and made every preparation to make a favorable impression. Although the admiral declined the honor of dining, owing to the fact that he would have to meet the ambassador from Algiers, who had not been accredited, he came on board with a large retinue in great splendor late in the afternoon.

The ship was covered with bunting, the yardarms were manned, and the crew were dressed in clean white uniforms. The Capudan Pasha was delighted with everything he saw. He remarked with great approbation the correct deportment of the officers, and praised highly the discipline and subordination of the crew. He was amazed at the structure of the ship, the heaviness of her bulwarks, and the strength of her timbers; for, mind you, he looked at her with a sailor's eye. But most he marveled at the cleanliness and neatness that prevailed throughout. He regretted frankly that such a state of things would never be found on board a Turkish vessel, and humorously expressed it that he was afraid his junior officers would see no use in such carefulness and attention to detail.

Before he left he invited Bainbridge and his first lieutenant to dine with him at his palace on the next day but one.

Although this was not a state function, and there were but seven seated at the table, the dinner was of great importance, as Bainbridge learned that the embassy which he had been at such pains to bring thither was not to be accredited at all. The presents of silks and satins, the lion cubs, and the Arabian steeds were all to be returned whence they came.

"What message the Grand Seignior intends to send to the Dey of Algiers has not yet been determined upon, but the Sultan has expressed the greatest displeasure at the conduct of Algiers, and will probably demand of him immediate reparation for the depredations he has committed on the commerce of Austria and other friendly nations, and also for his disobedience in making peace with France, our enemy."

Bainbridge then told of the insolent demand of the Dey that he should fly the Algerine flag. When he heard of this, the Pasha frowned.

"While in Ottoman waters," he said at last, "pray fly no flag but that of your own country, and as upon your return voyage you will still be under my protection, I respectfully request that you do not fly any other but that which is now at the peak of your vessel."

Altogether the dinner was a great success. The great English traveler, Edward Daniel Clarke, who had traveled to Constantinople from St. Petersburg in Russia over-

The Turkish admiral visits the Washington.

land by the way of Moscow and Odessa, was one of the guests. He was the first foreigner to make this long and hazardous journey.

This was by no means the last of the meetings between the admiral and the American captain. Visits were exchanged on many occasions, and several long excursions were made into the surrounding country and up the Thracian Bosporus, Bainbridge penetrating in his long boat even as far as the Black Sea, where he wished to hoist the American flag for the first time. He was also fortunate enough to secure a nearer view of the private and social life of the Turkish ruler than has fallen to the lot of many men, for Mr. Clarke one day presented him to Count Browlaski, a Pole in the service of the Sultan, a high officer in the court circle, and one who had immediate supervision of the gardens and the policing of the palace grounds.

Bainbridge had expressed a desire to see the inside of the seraglio and the harem, whose many grated windows looked down upon the blue waters of the bay from above the palace walls. The Englishman at once laughed and shrugged his shoulders.

"That speech shows your innocence, Captain Bainbridge," he said. "No one, not even our friend the count here, has had that privilege."

At this Count Browlaski looked over his shoulder, and observing that no one was nigh them, he confided to them that if they wished to run a certain amount of risk he thought the adventure might be carried out. Accordingly plans were arranged, and the visit was successfully accomplished. Mr. Clarke, in his book of travels, mentions meeting Captain Bainbridge, and going with him into the inner recesses of the palace in disguise. He dwells at some length upon the dangers that were encountered, but in a letter to a friend of his, Bainbridge made light of them in describing the same event. But he added generously, upon reading Mr. Clarke's account: "One gentleman may honestly apprehend great peril where it can not be perceived by another."

In return for all the courtesies that had been shown him, Bainbridge gave a large entertainment in the cabin of the George Washington. Although the admiral again declined the honor of being present, he was represented unofficially by Mr. Zaebe, his secretary. The disgruntled Algerine ambassador was also present. He was a man of grave deportment and good manners, and Bainbridge had begun to feel really sorry for him, owing to the failure of his mission, and the consequences that it might entail upon him and his family, for eastern vengeance does not stop at the principles involved in trouble or disgrace.

It was a remarkable entertainment in more ways than one. Upon the four corners of the table were so many decanters containing fresh water from the four quarters of the globe. The natives of Europe, Asia, Africa, and America sat down together at one board. Fruits, preserved dishes and viands were passed about—a sample of four different continents. In writing of this affair, Mr. Clarke explains it thus: "The means of accomplishing this extraordinary entertainment is easily understood by his (Bainbridge's) having touched at Algiers in his passage from America, and his being at anchor so near the shores of both Europe and of Asia."

Two more very important interviews Bainbridge held with the Capudan Pasha. The first was in answer to a request to know how long it would be expected of him to stay in port, and whether it would be necessary for him to return the embassy which had made such a fruitless journey. The admiral's reply to the first was that he did not think Bainbridge would now be detained longer than four or five days at the outside, but he requested especially that he would return the ambassador and his suite, who had not been permitted to land since their arrival in the harbor.

As Bainbridge had had many conversations with the Pasha on the subject of a treaty of commerce with the Ottoman Government, he could not very well refuse. But this was not the only subject of discussion at the meeting. A few minutes previous to Bainbridge's taking his departure the Turkish admiral had incidentally observed that he had not been a little surprised to learn on his return to the port that the American frigate had not been subjected to the usual restraints of the Dardanelles.

"I assure you, Monsieur le Capitaine, that it is the first time a foreign armored vessel has reached this port without our express permission and a firman from the Grand Seignior—Oh, do not apologize," he added, seeing that Bainbridge was about to speak. "I attach no blame whatever to your honorable conduct. You are a stranger to the laws and customs of this country and could not be expected to know our rules and regulations. But," he added, frowning, "it was, nevertheless, the governor of the castle's duty to stop you at the Dardanelles, even if, alas! he had to sink the fine vessel which you have the honor to command. He is not to escape punishment for this obvious breach of duty, for he is at present under sentence of death for his dereliction. It requires but my signature, and that, I promise you, shall not be withheld. He dies the day after to-morrow at sundown."

Bainbridge drew back in horror. The idea of allowing an innocent man to suffer for a doing of his own was more than his just mind and noble nature could brook for an instant. No matter what the consequences might be, he would make a statement.

"I assure your highness that the governor of the castle at the straits is not even censurable for his conduct. Believe me, it was through no fault of his that my vessel came by him."

The Capudan Pasha smiled and shrugged his shoulders.

"He should have stopped you at all hazards, Monsieur," he said. "Pray explain how any vessel could pass those powerful batteries upon which the safety of this city depends without gross neglect on the part of the commander of the castle."

"But he was not neglectful." Bainbridge spoke almost loudly now in his eagerness to convince the admiral of his sincerity.—"He was not neglectful. He imagined that I was coming to anchor. I frankly confess to you that I did everything in my power to deceive him into thinking that I was going to comply with the requirements of the port, for I knew well of the custom, and determined to evade it, if I could, to avoid delay. If any one should be punished it should be myself. But I trust that you will consider the circumstances and my haste to perform the mission that I had so unwillingly undertaken."

Bainbridge had no idea what would be the effect of this remarkable statement. The surprise of the admiral was plain at the outset, but as Bainbridge proceeded, the frown gradually left his face to be replaced by one of friendly amazement, and when the captain had finished speaking, the Pasha extended his hand.

"Thanks, a thousand times, for your brave words, my friend," he said. "The Governor was an old and trusted friend of mine. I now believe him to have been a faithful officer. I thank you from my heart again for saving me much pain, and preserving to the service of the Sultan a loyal servant. Do not fear that the words you have said shall cause you to suffer in any way. To-night one of my swiftest sailing boats will leave bearing the message that the governor is pardoned and restored to his former authority."

An English ship was about sailing for the port of Gibraltar, and by her Bainbridge sent the following letter, with a request to the captain to place it on board the first vessel bound for the United States. The epistle was addressed to his Excellency the Secretary of the Navy of the United States, and read as follows:

"SIR: On the 23d of December, 1801, I was requested by the Capudan Pasha to wait upon him at his palace. I was received in a very friendly manner, and had some conversation respecting the formation of a treaty with the Ottoman Porte, and he expressed a very great desire that a minister should be sent from the United States to effect it. I informed him that there was one already named, who at present was in Lisbon, and probably would be here in six months. He said he would write to the ambassador, which letter would be a protection for him while in the Turkish Empire, and gave me liberty to recommend any merchant vessel to his protection which might wish to come here previously to the arrival of the ambassador. I thanked him in the name of the United States for the protection he had been pleased to give the frigate under my command, and for his friendly attentions to myself and officers. I conceive it to be a very fortunate moment to negotiate an advantageous treaty with this Government. . . . The Capudan Pasha requested me to take two messengers and land them at Malta, being destined for Tripoli and Tunis, which I have consented to do, conceiving it to be good policy. I think it very probable that the States of Barbary will shortly receive chastisement from the Turks."

The ambassador of the Dey requested the honor of an interview with Bainbridge the next morning. He was found in a towering rage, and was almost unintelligible, as he tried to explain that at last the Grand Seignior had condescended to answer him. He said he was directed to return at once to Algiers, which country was ordered to immediately declare war against France; his master, the Dey, was to be compelled to pay the large sum of one million of piastres, and that only sixty days were to be allowed for the transmitting of this dispatch to Algiers and for an answer to be returned to Constantinople. If this time was exceeded war would be at once declared on Algiers.

The ambassador begged and implored Bainbridge to make haste and leave the shores of Turkey behind him. All his airs of superiority and importance disappeared. He was a frightened, cringing, and well-nigh hopeless creature whose ruin stared him in the face. As Bainbridge had been requested to wait upon the Capudan Pasha the next morning, it was impossible for him to leave until this was complied with; but yielding to the importunities of the frightened ambassador, he sent a messenger to the palace, asking that he should be allowed to see the admiral in the afternoon in order that he might sail at daybreak the next morning. Word came back that the Pasha would be glad to see him.

After presenting Bainbridge with a letter addressed to the Honorable William Smith, minister plenipotentiary of the United States at the port of Lisbon, the admiral turned with a great deal of courtesy and said the following words in parting:

"As your ship has been under my protection, she shall receive the honors that are reserved exclusively for my flag. In passing the fortress of Tapana it will salute you, which, of course, you will return."

By regulation this fortress saluted no one but the Capudan Pasha, and the compliment had never before been extended to any foreign vessel of war, nor even to Turkish vessels commanded by a less personage than an admiral; but, what was more important, Bainbridge bore away with him passports for the George Washington which entitled that vessel and her commander at all times to greatest respect in Turkish ports, and from all ships of that empire.

The officer at the Dardanelles, who had been restored to his command, sensible of the gallant conduct of Bainbridge, invited him to his castle, and in the most feeling manner thanked him for having saved his life when he had given up all hope and made his last will, excepting surely to perish. He insisted upon presenting the frigate with almost a cargo of fresh provisions and fruit, and he parted from the captain with renewed assurances of endless gratitude.

CHAPTER X.

It was the 21st of January, 1801, when the George Washington arrived again off Algiers, but Bainbridge had profited by the lesson he had learned, and he brought his ship to anchor outside of the mole and beyond the range of the harbor batteries.

As soon as he had appeared, two large sailboats put out to meet him; one contained Mr. O'Brien and the other a representative of the Dey, and it was a race to see which one would arrive first. O'Brien's sailboat, however, caught a bad current by keeping too close to the shore, and the regent's boat was the first alongside. Bainbridge received the court officer without much ceremony, and was rather amused to notice that the effect of seeing the returned embassy depressed the very consequential individual.

Before he had asked any questions of his countryman, he hastened to deliver a message for his master, in the following words: "His High Mightiness the Dey has noticed at what distance the honorable captain has dropped anchor, and he expresses great solicitude that immediately the frigate should be moved nearer the city. It surely must be inconvenient, his High Mightiness fears, for the officers to have communication with the shore."

As the messenger was still speaking O'Brien came on board.

"Listen to the blackguard!" he exclaimed, after

greeting Bainbridge. "Listen to the palvering old scamp!"

"He would have me under the guns of his fortress again if he could," Bainbridge said, half smiling; "but he won't get me there so easily this time."

"I see you've returned the menagerie," commented O'Brien.

"Yes, and I'll be glad to be rid of them," said Bainbridge, watching the preparations that were being made for the Moslems to leave the ship.

Indeed it was a great relief when the last one had gone over the side, and were it not for one thing, the American captain would have made all haste to get away. But previous to sailing he had taken aboard as ballast a large number of old iron cannon, which he promised to return, and he felt himself in duty bound to do so. And so he called away his gig, and, accompanied by the consul, he rowed into the harbor, intending to obtain an interview with the Dey; but again he was disappointed in securing a direct audience, and had to be content carrying on a species of verbal correspondence through the medium of one of the court officials.

Bainbridge had allowed Mr. O'Brien to begin the negotiations, but the Dey's reply to the usual formal greetings showed his position clearly. Point-blank he made the request to the consul general to order Bainbridge to return at once with his messenger to Constantinople. Bainbridge, upon hearing this, could not contain his indignation. Whirling suddenly, he advanced upon the astonished minister and in loud tones delivered himself of the following speech, while poor Mr. O'Brien almost collapsed in a state of fright, fearing the result of his friend's temerity:

"Tell your master," Bainbridge said fiercely to the interpreter, "that he has forgotten the oath he swore not to make any further demands upon me after the first voyage was performed. Now, in the face of such a solemn declaration, he makes another insolent request. Any one who thus proves his unworthiness should be denied all credence. Tell him I do not doubt his disposition to capture my frigate and enslave my officers and crew. To preserve peace I complied with his first demand. I have done everything which the commander of a ship would be justified in doing to prevent hostilities; but, mark you, if the Dey is determined to have war, if he is so mad as to make the Americans his enemy, he soon will have cause to regret it."

With these words Bainbridge beckoned for the consul to follow him, and stalked out of the palace. In addition to the letter which has been quoted, Bainbridge had written another one to the Secretary of the Navy saying that he anticipated a demand of this character, but giving assurance that he intended to resist it, "believing that the Government of the United States would never sanction an act so humiliating."

The following morning he requested from Mr. O'Brien that he send lighters off to the ship to receive the old cannon; but the Dey, hearing of this, not only forbade the consul making use of lighters, but declared that in the event of the guns not being returned at once, war would immediately be made upon the United States.

The consul, much frightened, asked Bainbridge to settle matters by running his ship into the mole and delivering up the cannon. Bainbridge refused to do this until he had received a positive promise from the Dey that he should not be approached upon the subject of a second voyage. Reluctantly this was given, but there was to be a dramatic scene in consequence. When Bainbridge came ashore after seeing that the cannon were hoisted over the side on to the dock, he was met by a court official accompanied by some thirty or forty armed janizaries, and word was given him that the Dey requested his presence on a matter of the utmost importance.

Leaving orders with his first lieutenant to begin at once to warp the ship out into the harbor and set sail if he did not return within two hours, taking with him only a midshipman, Bainbridge waited upon "his High Mightiness" at the palace and found him in a towering rage.

"Dog of a Christian, down on your knees!" shrieked the Dey, pointing to the floor at his feet. "Down, I say!" he continued, jumping up as he noticed that Bainbridge's only reply was a calm folding of his arms and a more erect carriage to his figure, in every motion of which the little midshipman accompanied him.

The Dey was absolutely foaming and spluttering in his wrath. He drew his long curved scimiter, and at the motion the crowd of armed men drew theirs also. The minutes that Bainbridge and his little companion had to live seemed numbered, when suddenly the captain thought of the firman that he had thrust in his pocket a minute before he had left shipboard. Not having the least idea of what the result would be he drew it forth. At sight of the document, with its two ponderous seals, the Dey's jaw dropped, and sheathing his weapon, he fell back timorously before Bainbridge, who, backed up by the unflinching little middy, advanced upon him, unrolling the document and displaying it triumphantly for the Dey's inspection. Only in the Arabian Nights could any one read of such transformations being enacted. It was as if he had pronounced some magic word—some open sesame—whose power was resistless. With a weak motion to his astonished court the Dey bade them withdraw, and, to the American captain's wonderment, he found confronting him, not an arrogant, bloodthirsty tyrant, but a cringing, humble dependent, alone but for a single dragoman who had prostrated himself upon the floor. Almost abjectly he requested the honor of having the American captain sit down beside him on the divan. As Bainbridge wrote, "his bearing became less lofty, his words honeyed, and his offers of service most liberal."

The Dey cut down the flagstaff before the French consulate, declared war against France, and made preparations to send an installment of the money demanded by the Sultan, amounting to one million five hundred thousand piastres, and humble apology thrown in, to Turkey.

By orders of the Sultan also he had been compelled to liberate about four hundred Venetians, Maltese, and Sicilians, whom he had taken prisoners when they were traveling under the protection of British passports. All these people hailed Bainbridge as their generous deliverer.

Just before he was ready to sail, it was rumored that the citizens of the French Republic, fifty-six in number, consisting of men, women, and children, had been by the Dey's orders thrown into chains and treated as slaves. Bainbridge and Mr. O'Brien waited upon the Dey, and expressed to him their ideas about such treatment.

"All right," the Dey returned; "then they must leave Algiers in forty-eight hours."

"There are no vessels ready to convey us. Grant us more time," prayed Monsieur Dubois de Trainville, who was present at the interview.

"Our countries are now at war," he added, turning to Bainbridge; "but I beseech you, for the cause of humanity, to take me and the other French prisoners aboard of your ship."

But the consul had only anticipated Bainbridge's own desire, the captain giving up his own cabin for the use of the ladies, and supplying them all with the necessities for the voyage, for the poor French people left Algiers in such a hurry that they had time to procure nothing but the clothes they wore.

The George Washington, bidding farewell to Algiers, set sail for France, and after a short passage arrived safely at Alicante. The gratitude of the people whom he had saved was unbounded, and Napoleon, at that time first

Alicante.

consul, tendered his "acknowledgments and thanks to Captain Bainbridge for the important services he had rendered the republic, with assurances that such kind offices would always be remembered, and reciprocated with pleasure whenever occasion offered."

From Alicante, Bainbridge set sail for America, and after explaining and reporting to the President in person, the latter expressed his approbation, and even commended him for the judicious and skillful manner in which he had discharged his duty while under the pressure of such extraordinary circumstances.

A historian, writing contemporaneously of these times, says as follows: "This humiliating condition in which Captain Bainbridge was placed arose out of the feeble policy of our Government in stipulating to purchase an immunity from insult to our citizens, and spoliations on our commerce by paying an annual tribute to barbarians whom it could have readily controlled by force. There is no other way of giving complete protection to our citizens and to our property afloat than by 'the cannon's mouth.' Dearly-bought experience has proved the utter fallacy of Mr. Jefferson's scheme of preserving peace by pursuing a pacific and upright policy toward all nations. The point is now settled, however, that nothing less than an exhibition of force and willingness to exercise it can maintain unimpaired our national rights and dignity."

Indeed, it is most remarkable when we think that the United States could have so long put up with this condition of affairs. There were many who saw that it could end but one way, and advocated a very different line of action. Among these was the young officer who, at the age of twenty-six, had conducted himself with such a display of knowledge and judgment. It was safe to assert that he would answer for himself in the event of troublous times.

CHAPTER XI.

It was Bainbridge's good fortune to find his wife and all his relations well. Another happy reunion was held at Middletown. But in the latter part of May a long envelope was handed to him, which he read to all those grouped about the table, from the Secretary of the Navy, and couched in the following terms: "Appreciating highly your character as an officer, the President has selected you to command the frigate Essex, and has placed the whole squadron under the command of Commodore Richard Dale, to whose orders he enjoins you to pay strict attention and due obedience."

As the Essex was then in New York, Bainbridge joined her at once, and found that the squadron preparing for sea consisted of the President, flagship of Commodore Dale; the Philadelphia, under command of Captain Barron; his own vessel the Essex; and the schooner Enterprise, under command of Commandant Sterrett. It was intended that these ships should proceed to the Mediterranean to protect American commerce, with whose interests the Bashaw of Tripoli had seen fit to interfere. Bainbridge was rejoiced to go on this expedition, and delighted that he should have been honored with the command of so fine a vessel as the Essex. He was most fortunate to have under him a fine body of young officers and seamen. His first lieutenant was a man of character and determination; there was not much difference in their ages, and his name was Stephen Decatur.

After a pleasant voyage, the squadron arrived at Gibraltar on the 1st of July, where two large Tripolitan corsairs were found at anchor. The Philadelphia was detailed to watch the movements of the Tripolitans, while the Essex was dispatched to Marseilles, Barcelona, Alicante, and other ports on the coast, for the purpose of collecting the American merchant fleet, preparatory to escorting it through the Strait of Gibraltar.

Barcelona was the first port visited. The Yankee frigate was received with a great deal of courtesy, and all went well for the first few days, until the officers of a Spanish guard ship, angered and jealous because of the comments of their countrymen in comparing their own craft with that of the Americans, decided to make it disagreeable for officers going on shore or passing off to the vessel. So they stopped three or four boats and insulted the officers. The morning after this occurrence Decatur rowed to the Spaniard, and demanded to see the officer in command—intending to challenge him, for duels were then common occurrences. When he was told that the lieutenant he was after had gone ashore, he left the following message for him, to be given to him on his return: "Tell the man who threatened to fire into an unarmed boat's crew that Lieutenant Decatur, of the Essex, denounces him as a cowardly scoundrel, and when they meet on shore he will cut his ears off."

Luckily, however, no meeting took place, for it is without doubt that Lieutenant Decatur would have done his best to carry out his threat.

It might be unfair to leave the subject, however, without stating that the insolent Spanish officer was compelled to apologize.

Sailing from Barcelona with a large fleet of merchantmen that had been collected in the various harbors of the Mediterranean, the Essex saw them safely outside of the strait and returned to Gibraltar, where it was learned that the Tripolitan corsairs had been successfully cooped up and been dismantled by the Philadelphia, and the crews sent over to Africa in small boats by night, to make their way to Tripoli across the desert, while the Tripolitan admiral had taken passage in an English vessel bound for Malta.

Bainbridge cruised in different parts of the Mediterranean during the winter and spring, and showed himself off the cities of Tunis, Algiers, and Tripoli.

The Essex needing repairs, she was ordered to return home, where she arrived in July, 1802.

In the harbor of New York there was a little trouble with the crew, who insisted upon being discharged and paid off, as their time had expired; but, owing to Bainbridge's promptness, a mutiny was averted and the frigate proceeded at once to Washington, and after some delay reached the navy yard early in August, where she was dismantled in order to make the necessary repairs.

Bainbridge, who had removed his family to Philadelphia, was not loath to receive orders for shore duty as soon as his leave of absence was up. He was connected with the Ordnance Department, and superintended the building of the brig Siren and the schooner Vixen. It was not till the 21st of May, 1803, that he received sailing orders, and was given the command of the frigate Philadelphia, forty-four guns.

She was soon ordered attached to the squadron of Commodore Preble, consisting of the flagship Constitution of forty-four guns; the brig Siren of twelve guns, under command of Captain Stewart; the schooner Vixen of fourteen guns, Lieutenant-Commandant J. Smith; the Argus of sixteen guns, under command of Lieutenant-Commandant I. Hull; the Nautilus of twelve guns, Lieutenant-Commander R. Somers; Enterprise of twelve guns, commanded by Lieutenant-Commandant Stephen Decatur. The whole expedition was fitted out with the intention of cruising in the Mediterranean, but as it would be some time before they would all be ready, Bainbridge received orders on the 13th of July to proceed with his frigate, the Philadelphia, in advance of the others, and, under the authority of an act of Congress, to subdue, seize, and make prize of all vessels, goods, and effects belonging to the Bashaw of Tripoli or his subjects, who had declared war against the United States.

Once more Bainbridge found under his orders a fine body of officers. Their names have since become known to history. David Porter was his first lieutenant, Jacob Jones his second, Theodore Hunt and Benjamin Smith, his third and fourth, respectively. Among the midshipmen we find James Biddle, Robert Gamble, James Renshaw, and D. T. Patterson.

On the 26th of August the Philadelphia was off Cabo de Gata, a promontory on the coast of Spain. It

Location of Ports in the Mediterranean.

was blowing very fresh, and only a mile or so distant was seen a large ship carrying only her foresail, and just astern of her was a little brig, evidently in her company. It was so dark that it was impossible to determine the character of either vessel; but at early daybreak they were quite near to hand, and it was perceived that the ship was heavily armed, although all of her guns were housed. Her appearance was suspicious, as her decks swarmed with swarthy men, and she displayed no flag.

Without stating who he was, Bainbridge hailed her, and ordered her to send a boat and one of her officers on board of him at once. The fact that the brig was so close to the other almost confirmed him in his suspicions that she was a prize. The officer who boarded the Philadelphia in obedience to the command was dressed in European costume and spoke both French and Spanish. He denied that the brig was a prize, but confessed that she was an American, and had been with them four or five days, but was not in any way detained. He stated that his own ship was a Moorish cruiser of twenty-two guns and carrying one hundred and twenty men; that she belonged to the Emperor of Morocco; that her name was the Meshboha; and that she was commanded by Ibrahim Lubarez.

Lieutenant Porter rowed off to the ship in order to see if there were any American prisoners on board, but Captain Lubarez prevented his boarding, and as this increased Bainbridge's suspicion, he sent a boat filled with armed men to enforce his commands.

But let the story be told in Captain Bainbridge's own words: " No opposition was offered to this force; they (the boat's crew) found Captain Richard Rowen, of the American brig Cecilia, owned by Amasa Thayer, of Boston, and seven of his crew, who were taken on the 17th of August, twenty-five miles eastward of Malaga, whither they were bound. The Moors confined them under deck, which they always do when speaking a vessel the character of which is not known. The Moorish captain displayed a passport that had been obtained from the

United States consul at Tangiers, and, on seeing this, Bainbridge had no hesitation in making all on board prisoners because of the violation of faith.

"The Americans were taken off and placed back on their own vessel, and allowed to depart for Malaga. The morning after the capture, Bainbridge held a conversation at some length with Ibrahim. He asked him why he should so violate all rules of honor by capturing the vessel of a friendly nation while sailing under her passport. The wily Mohammedan said at first that his sole reason was the fact that he supposed his country and the United States would soon be at war."

"Is that the truth?" questioned Bainbridge, upon hearing this.

The Moor signified assent.

"Then, sir," returned Bainbridge sternly, "I must consider you a pirate, and will be obliged to treat you as such. If in one quarter of an hour your authority for preying upon the commerce of the United States is not forthcoming, I'll hang you to yonder main yardarm as a malefactor."

With that he sent the trembling wretch into the cabin under guard, and in a quarter of an hour he had him brought on deck. A rope was wove with a noose at the end of it, and one glance at that and his captor's determined countenance, and the Moor's knees began to tremble. Hastily he unbuttoned several waistcoats, and from the inside pocket of the fifth he drew out a document. It was a paper signed by the Emperor of Morocco authorizing the capture of American vessels. This saved the Moor's life, and the paper was sent to Commodore Preble at Gibraltar. It was a discovery of great importance.

After discovering that the captain of the Meshboha was not acting on his own responsibility, but really under orders of his Government, Bainbridge treated him with great courtesy, and also gave orders to treat the other prisoners not as pirates but as prisoners of war, and one of the Philadelphia's own seamen was punished for striking one of the Moorish sailors.

Bainbridge now made sail for Cape St. Vincent, hearing that a Moorish thirty-gun ship was cruising in that quarter. The search for her was unsuccessful, and he returned to the Mediterranean to cruise off Tripoli.

In a few days Commodore Preble arrived, and as soon as he had learned of the proceedings he set sail for Tangiers and demanded instant reparation from the Emperor of Morocco. The Emperor said that the Moorish cruisers had not sailed under his orders but under those of the Governor of Tangiers, and he at once made a scapegoat of the latter, although it is perfectly apparent that he was really the author of the whole trouble.

Commodore Preble thanked Bainbridge officially and in person for his vigilance and foresight, and Congress voted afterward prize money to the value of the Moorish vessel to be divided among the crew.

CHAPTER XII.

BAINBRIDGE was sitting in his cabin late one morning looking over some maps when Lieutenant Porter stopped at the cabin door.

"Well, Mr. Porter," said Captain Bainbridge, looking up and smiling, "come in. Did you wish to speak to me?"

"Yes, sir," replied Porter, entering. "You remember the news that the captain of the Neapolitan merchant brig gave us the day before yesterday, saying that a Tripolitan brig had just sailed out for a cruise."

"Indeed I do," cried the captain eagerly. "Did the Vixen capture her? She could not have been far behind."

"No," Porter answered; "but there is a strange sail, evidently a Tripolitan, standing close inshore."

"Let's up and have a look at her," Bainbridge laughed, jamming his heavy hat down upon his brows. "I think a little excitement would do us good. How's the wind?"

"About due east, sir."

It was nine o'clock, for two bells were struck just as the captain and the lieutenant returned on deck. The former took a squint through the telescope at the white sail inshore and then turned hurriedly.

"It is the cruiser; I'd almost swear to it," he exclaimed. "Make all sail, and take after her. We are but six or seven leagues to the east of Tripoli, and, by George!

we'll head her off. We've got all the water we wish under our keel; let's put our best foot forward."

There was much bustle and bawling as the Philadelphia broke out her studding sails and spread her royals, and slowly she began to creep up upon the chase, that was no mean sailer by the way, and had spread a great lanteen sail forward that stretched almost to the water's edge over her bulwarks. In a few minutes over an hour the corsair was in within long range, and as it was perceived that she was armed, Bainbridge began to fire at her with his forward division; most of the balls fell short, but the firing did not interfere in the least with the other's attempt to get away. In fact she seemed to increase her speed, and did not make a response, although the long-range practice was kept up until half-past eleven. By this time the entrance to the harbor was in full view, and it became apparent that to reach there in advance of the other vessel was an impossibility.

Bainbridge and Porter had made frequent observation of the chart, and the deep-sea and the hand lead had been busy. The soundings ran from seven fathoms to ten, and the chart showed clear water up to the harbor's mouth. Reluctantly Bainbridge gave orders to take in sail and abandon the chase. The foresail was dropped, the helm was ordered hard aport, and the Philadelphia began to haul offshore. There was a strong current setting in toward the mouth of the harbor, but the wind was fresh, and soon the frigate had good headway on her.

"It is a shame to give up after getting so close up," grumbled Lieutenant Porter, noticing that the corsair had taken in her sails, evidently satisfied that she had shown the big ship a clean pair of heels.

Bainbridge had picked up a glass and was squinting over the taffrail at the low-lying coast and the clustering white-walled houses and spires that marked the city of Tripoli.

"By George, sir, look at that fleet of small craft lying alongside the wall just inside the harbor!" he exclaimed, handing the glass to Porter.

"Not so very small," the lieutenant replied; "I should judge those vessels ranged from thirty to ninety tons or more. They are the craft which do the most damage to our shipping—pirates, every man-jack of them!"

No sooner had he finished speaking than Bainbridge made a quick spring forward. He had been listening to the monotonous voice of the man heaving the lead, and the last sounding had filled him with a sudden consternation. Eight fathoms—and the next heave seven!—it was impossible, but he was not the only one who was listening.

"Plash!" went the lead.

"By the mark, six!" roared the man in the fore chains, changing his sing-song to a shrill, frightened tone.

Such an abrupt shoaling meant nothing less than immediate danger. The maps had shown safe water, but there was no gainsaying the testimony of the lead.

"Port your helm!" roared Bainbridge, twirling, and letting go the words at the quartermaster as if he was firing off a pistol.

The yards were braced about sharply as the vessel answered to her helm, but the Philadelphia had been running at the rate of five or six knots. It was hard to stop such headway, and it seemed hardly a breathing space between the time of the first order and the moment that a sudden shock was felt, followed by an upward lifting motion as the bow raised itself, and then by a grinding, crunching sound that showed the timbers below were undergoing some frightful strain. Bainbridge uttered no exclamation. He exchanged a glance with Porter that meant much, however—a combined look of astonishment and distress. But no fear showed in the face of either, although it was a moment to frighten the stoutest hearts.

Where had the reef come from? It was as if some enemy of the deep had suddenly raised up to crush the vessel in its spiteful jaws.

The watch below had come pouring up on deck; but seeing their commander calmly giving orders from the quarter-deck, and their companions scrambling aloft to lay the sails aback in obedience to his commands, without the least confusion they followed suit, going to their stations as quietly as if it were fire drill instead of a sudden danger they had to face.

Lieutenant Jones, who had gone forward to the forecastle, sent Midshipman Biddle hurrying aft.

"There's not fourteen feet below us at the fore channels, sir!" he said breathlessly, saluting Bainbridge, who saw to his dismay that the sails were not working the vessel off in the slightest.

The next order was to run aft all the guns of the forward division in the hope of raising the bow until she should be clear of the rocks. The trunnions roared and grumbled as the sailors bustled the heavy, clumsy guns down the sloping deck until they were all huddled well abaft the mainmast.

"Has she lifted, sir?" asked Bainbridge of Lieutenant Jones.

"Not an inch, sir," was the answer.

Matters indeed looked bad.

"Cut away both those anchors, Mr. Biddle," Bainbridge thundered.

A few blows with an axe and the four tons of iron plashed from either side of the bows. Still she did not move. The sails aloft were drawing well. It was a remarkable sight. With a cross-current and quite a sea running outside, the leach of the mainsail romping and flapping, and yet the deck of the ship as steady as the floor of a courthouse. It produced an uncanny, frightened feeling that seized upon the heart; it was an unnatural thing to watch—if any one could have stopped to watch it; but there was not time for that; every man was on the jump.

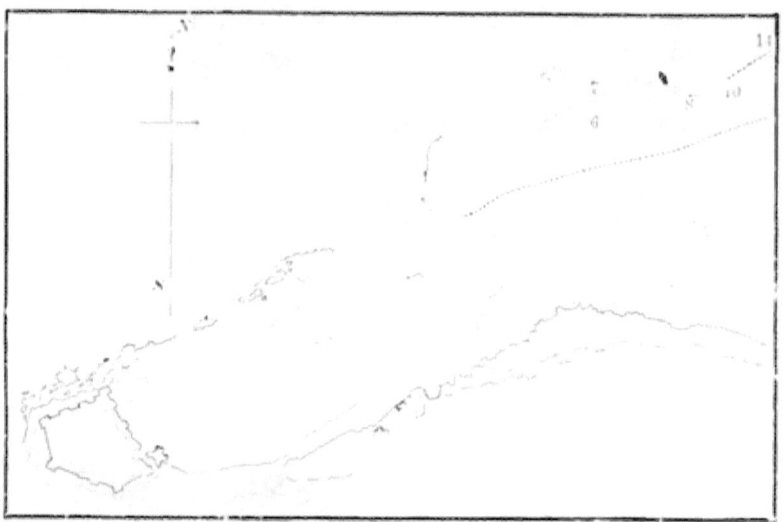

Diagram explaining the loss of the Philadelphia.
Tripoli and the castle on the left; figures indicating fathoms on the right.

"Where's the carpenter? Send the carpenter aft to me," said Bainbridge quietly to Midshipman Robert Gamble.

The middy ran below. "Godley, you're wanted on the quarter-deck," he cried to a tall seaman into whose arms he almost fell. "Captain wants to speak to you. Lively there! Don't stop."

The carpenter went up the ladder in three jumps; in two more he was at the break of the poop.

"Get ten men and stave in those forward water casks— every one of them."

Off went the carpenter, plunging down the companion way.

"Bo'sun," roared Bainbridge, catching sight of Boatswain George Hadger hurrying across the deck, "is there any water in the well?"

"No, sir," the old seaman cried, saluting; "and it's just been sounded. She's tight and dry, sir."

"Rig the pumps, then, and get this fresh water overboard."

In three minutes the steady "slish, slosh, click, clack" of the big pumps sounded throughout the ship, and the water from the springs of Pennsylvania poured out into the scuppers. Below, the carpenter and his crew could be heard assailing the stout ribs of the water casks.

But the old frigate did not lift her nose a single inch, and now a new danger appeared. Bainbridge, following the pointing arm of a man on the forecastle, turned around, but it was only for an instant. He had seen enough, however. Out from the mouth of the harbor was pouring the Tripolitan fleet; their pointed, white sails—scores of them—gleamed in the sunlight. If the Philadelphia could not be wore off before they arrived within gunshot her chances were slim indeed.

The majority of the crew on deck, hidden by the bulwarks, were ignorant of the new terror.

"Ask Mr. Porter to step here quickly," said Bainbridge to one of the midshipmen; and at the same time he gave an order that to an inexperienced ear might have seemed a strange one under the circumstances. It was a desperate resort—nothing less than to cast overboard all the guns that could be loosened; and soon almost the entire starboard battery had been put over the side.

The forward division on the port hand followed suit.

"Look there, Mr. Porter," said Bainbridge, nodding his head backward at the approaching fleet. "Cast loose and provide the stern chasers here, and run two of those heavy guns into my cabin. Break out the stern gallery. There's where they will take position. Has she moved?"

"Not an inch, sir," replied Porter firmly. "We'll have to fight for it."

Suddenly the boom of a gun sounded—the leading Tripolitan had commenced firing! Before five minutes had passed four large gunboats had taken their station under the larboard quarter. Splinters now began to fly, and the ripping and tearing aloft showed that the enemy's shot were crippling the yards and spars. Already three or four men, red and gory, had been carried below. The quarter-deck, on which Bainbridge was standing, was quivering from the discharge of the carronades that had been trundled into the cabin. Sulphur smoke was in the air, but the men were not cheering. They were fighting with a sullen determination.

A big boatswain's mate, serving one of the after guns, was standing upright, motioning the men with the handspikes how to slue the piece. With the one hand he was trying to stop the flow of blood from a great splinter wound in his breast. But before the piece could be fired the frigate gave a lurch, her bow rose a few feet higher on the sunken reef, and the brave sailor pitched headlong to the deck.

"Help me to my pins!" he cried weakly, making frantic efforts to rise; but it was useless. Another pitch and the deck was at such an angle that even the able-bodied could scarcely keep their feet. But three guns now could be brought to bear, and the crushing sound of the Tripolitan broadsides became an uninterrupted roar. The balls were entering the hull from all directions. One came in the stern port, and, being deflected, crossed to the other side and back again, as a billiard ball would bound from the angles of a table. But the deadly splinters scattered in its wake. Not a sign of fear, however, was to be observed among the crew, although three fourths of them could do nothing but stand idly by.

"Cut away the foremast!" cried Bainbridge, making a trumpet of his hands.

With a crash the great pine timbers yielded to the strokes of the axes, and down came the towering sails, hampering the forward deck and covering the forecastle in a mass of billowing, fluttering canvas.

The hull was almost on her broadside now, and the main-topgallant mast was cut away, but no relief was afforded. The fine vessel was a wreck, and, almost safe from her few guns, the enemy were pouring in their unceasing fire.

Yet for an hour longer the frigate replied bravely.

"No white feathers here," said Midshipman Biddle to his friend Gamble. And it was a fact. Not a single skulker was there in the Philadelphia's crew.

"Word's been passed for the officers," said Gamble, pointing.

There, under the shelter of the poop, for the quarter-deck was now swept by a murderous fire, Bainbridge, with his three lieutenants, and William Knight, the master, were in consultation.

"I can not sacrifice the lives of my brave men longer," the captain said. "Gentlemen, I've done my best; for the cause of humanity we will have to strike."

It was a cruel fate. To strike his country's flag to a civilized foe after a hard-fought battle would have been gall and vinegar to the commander's high-strung nature; but to yield to this uncivilized and barbarous enemy was humiliating.

"Sir," said Porter, extending his hand, "we've all done our best, and we appreciate your feelings; but there is nothing for it."

The silence of the other officers made known their acquiescence.

"Tell the carpenter to scuttle the ship," Bainbridge said calmly. "Overboard with the small arms, Mr. Porter. See that the magazine is flooded—Mr. Jones, I am sorry, sir; haul down the flag!"

The proud emblem came slowly to the deck, the carronades ceased their useless replying to the enemy's well-directed fire. An unearthly, discordant yell broke from the line of the barbarians. A few of the smaller craft, that had just sailed into range, discharged their guns with screams of triumph, much as cowardly savages would fling their darts into the helpless body of some great beast that the real hunters had dispatched at their peril.

The men had been ordered to collect their dunnage and belongings; and to prevent a massacre, there was nothing to be done but to trust to the good temper of the victors. The officers searched everywhere for small arms, heaving them out of ports and over the bulwarks; this last operation was hardly completed before the first boat of the Tripolitan fleet gained the side. With shrill cries the dusky, turbaned Moslems swarmed aboard through the ports, and in an instant the ship was surrounded by the clamoring, screaming horde.

The scene that followed almost passes description. The sailors had retreated to the forecastle, where they were gathered in a compact body, held only in check by the calm words of the officers scattered among them.

"Steady, now, men," said Midshipman Biddle in an undertone; "make no resistance if you wish to save our lives."

As he spoke the midshipman gazed with calm eyes into the face of a bearded, swarthy pirate, who flourished a sharp scimiter within an inch of his throat. The men in the front rank, following their officer's example, folded their arms and stood erect. Not a sound broke from them, except a few curses as they perceived that the Tripolitans were not going to respect the laws of private property. Ditty-boxes and bags were broken into, and their contents scattered about and scrambled for on deck.

Suddenly the frigate settled a little at the stern, and it was remembered that the carpenter had been ordered to let the water into her. Obeying the commands of one or two who seemed to be in authority, and kept in order by their own officers, the men clambered over the side on to the deck of one of the large gunboats that lay grinding against the rail. It was a good thing that they had left just at this moment, for had they stayed they would never have been able to stand calmly by and watch what happened on the quarter-deck.

Bainbridge had been addressing in French and Italian the wild crowd that were looting the vessel, asking repeatedly for their leader—for some one to whom he could surrender his sword and from whom he could claim protection. But no one paid attention to him so intent were the fiends upon bringing everything of value up from below, for they feared that the ship might sink at any moment. The setting sun threw a red light across the scene. To leeward hung the white cloud of battle smoke, almost a mile distant by this time, and in the sharply defining rays the varied colors worn by the Tripolitans, shuffling and scampering on the main deck, stood out brightly, like the shifting tones of a kaleidoscope.

All at once the hubbub ceased for an instant as if they had just caught a glimpse of the tall, broad-shouldered figure looking down upon them from the quarter-deck. His three lieutenants stood but a few paces behind him, with set faces and firmly compressed lips. A great, heavily turbaned pirate shouted something, and climbed up the steps of the quarter-deck followed by a half-score of others, bearing their plunder underneath their arms, as if fearful of dropping it. Bainbridge advanced to meet the leader, extending the hilt of his sword as he did so. The cut-throat took it.

"Dog of a Christian!" he cried, making a vicious thrust at the middle of the captain's body. The point struck the heavy belt plate and glanced harmlessly, and the man drew back. Bainbridge was standing there with his arms folded and a smile upon his lips. The corsair lowered his arm; then he pointed with his finger at the heavy pistol in the American's belt. It was handed over, and Bainbridge, a moment later, gazed unflinchingly into it as the scoundrel pointed it directly at his head. The pistol was lowered.

Porter, who was standing but a few feet away, was about to spring, but his commander caught the movement.

"Steady, gentlemen!" he said; "your lives depend upon it. We must submit."

Insolently the Tripolitan leader stretched forth his hand and lifted one of the heavy gold epaulets from the captain's shoulder. Then he took the other, and picked the jeweled pin from his neckcloth. The crowd gathered in the waist had become silent spectators of these goings on, and following the example of the swarthy villain, some of his crew were despoiling the lieutenants in the same way. Calmly they submitted to the removal of their coats and waistcoats, and, without a tremor, allowed themselves to be robbed of their heavy fobs and watches. Bainbridge's eyes were following every movement of the man who was submitting him to this indignity. His flashing eyes contradicted the calm, contemptuous sneer upon his lips. One thought had entered his mind—a thought that brought a sickening fear in its wake. Lying upon his breast, suspended by a thin gold chain around his neck, was a miniature of Susan, his wife. Would he be able to

The miniature of Mrs. Bainbridge.
From the original, now in possession of the family.

stand calmly and watch it torn from him by those dirty, blood-stained hands? All at once the gleam of the gold chain caught the eye of the robber. With a swift motion he tore the soft linen shirt open at the throat. There lay the miniature, the calmly smiling face of a woman, in a white, high-waisted gown. With a greedy cry he reached for it, but his eager fingers never touched the shining gold. With a roar like a cornered beast that counts no odds, Bainbridge seized him by the throat. As he stood there no one could have failed to notice the tremendous muscles plain to view, but no one would have supposed that human arms possessed such strength. As one might beat a garment against a post to relieve it of clinging dust—yes, like a bundle of rags—he picked up that swarthy infidel and dashed him down against the rail. The man's skull cracked like an egg, and he fell limply down upon the heads of the crowd below.

Porter and Jones and Lieutenant Hunt sprang forward, but before they could gain their captain's side they were pinioned hard and fast. Bainbridge stood there panting. Some one fired a pistol at him at point-blank range, but, owing probably to the jostling of the crowd, the ball missed its mark. With a cry of rage five or six of the corsairs made at him. He felled the first one with a blow from his great fist, but they swarmed upon him almost too closely intertwined to draw their daggers. Again he struggled to his feet. With a mighty effort he grasped one of his assailants by his heavy cloth belt and whirled him overboard into the sea. Again they closed upon him. Their object now was to gain possession of the gleaming miniature. They had him down more than once, but could not force it from his grasp, although his fingers were torn and cut. It seemed to be ages that he struggled as if gifted with the strength of more than a dozen men. Time and again he rose to his knees only to be hauled down, like a fighting bull, by a pack of hungry wolves. For the fourth time he managed to stand erect and get his back against the rail. Unarmed, except in his magnificent strength, he stood there like a warrior of the stone age. The corsairs were almost awed at the sight of this man and the fight they had witnessed.

But a commotion suddenly began among those who had stood aloof as if waiting to see what the result would be. A handsomely dressed figure, in a briliant red tunic and silk scarf, was calling out to the others to make way for him. He gained the deck, and thrusting back the discomfited villains, he approached Bainbridge. The latter gathered himself as if for an onslaught, but the Moor bowed low before him, and turning so as to confront the others, he drew a long jewel-hilted pistol. No remonstrance was made to this action, and with great relief the officers, who had been almost weeping at their inability to help their leader, saw that here was one who held authority.

Calling again for a passageway to be cleared, he beckoned for the prisoners to follow him. Bainbridge, with the miniature still tightly grasped in his hand, almost breathless from the fearful struggle, motioned the other officers to precede him. Shorn of everything but his glory, he was the last to leave his ship.

CHAPTER XIII.

It was ten o'clock at night, some six hours after the surrender of the Philadelphia, that the prisoners were landed near the Bashaw's castle just as they were, except that the Tripolitan officer, who had saved Bainbridge, secured for him a makeshift suit of clothes. They were taken into the Bashaw's presence, where he sat in his audience hall on his divan, surrounded by his richly uniformed guards.

After having been subjected to a rigid cross-examination, and having replied to numerous questions, the party of officers were conducted to another apartment where a supper was served to them. At midnight they were taken back to the hall again and found that they had been placed in charge of the Minister of State, Sidi Mohammed Dgheis. This official proved to be a fine, dignified man of commanding presence, who was well acquainted with European manners and customs, and from the outset he not only enlisted the respect of his prisoners, but appeared anxious to do anything he could to serve them. He spoke excellent French, and informed them in the first words he spoke that he hoped to make their stay as little of a hardship as possible, and trusted on their word, if they would give it him, not to escape while under his immediate charge. Scarcely waiting for an answer, he dismissed the guard and bade them follow him. As he conducted them through the town, he told them that they were bound for the late American consul's house, which had been assigned to them as a temporary prison. Upon their arrival they found that the kind Tripolitan had also secured for them the clothing of which they had been despoiled—all but the epaulets and some of the ornamentation. He bade them good night after doing all he could for their comfort.

Poor Bainbridge was much depressed in spirit. He grieved at the loss of the new and beautiful frigate, and was apprehensive that his countrymen might censure him before the true cause of the disaster could be explained. There was one thing, however, that gave him comfort—it was the locket which he still wore upon his breast, and for which he would have laid down his life.

The next morning, not long after breakfast, Lieutenant Porter appeared at the captain's door.

"The compliments of the Philadelphia's officers to Captain Bainbridge," he said. "They beg that he will accept this paper which was prepared for his perusal."

Bainbridge opened it and read as follows:

TRIPOLI, *November 1, 1803.*

"SIR: We, late officers of the United States frigate Philadelphia, under your command, wish to express our full approbation of your conduct concerning the unfortunate event of yesterday, and do conceive that the charts and soundings justified as near an approach to the shore as we made; and that, after she struck, every expedient was tried to get her off and to defend her which either courage or abilities could have dictated.

"We wish to add that in this instance, as well as in every other, since we have had the honor of being under your command, the officers and seamen have always appreciated your distinguished conduct. Believe us, sir, that our misfortunes and sorrows are entirely absorbed in our sympathies for you. We are, sir, with sentiments of the highest and most sincere respect, your friends and fellow sufferers."

This paper was signed by all the lieutenants, midshipmen, officers, and petty officers from William Godley, the carpenter, to William Adams, the captain's clerk—twenty-seven signatures being appended.

But shortly after Bainbridge had received this letter, which caused him almost to break down, because of its kindness and honest feeling, the Minister of State was announced. With him was Mr. N. C. Nissen, whom he introduced to Bainbridge as his particular friend. Mr. Nissen was the Danish consul, and Sidi Mohammed took the opportunity to say he was the only consul in Tripoli for whom he had the least respect.

The Dane expressed great sympathy for Bainbridge in his misfortunes, and the American captain saw at a glance that he was a friend worth keeping. Mr. Nissen's manner satisfied all of the American officers that he was well entitled to the esteem that had been expressed for him by the Tripolitan minister. As soon as he had departed, Bainbridge asked for pen, ink, and paper, and, sitting down at the little table, the only bit of furniture the room possessed, he wrote the following letter to his wife, even before he indited the official notice he intended sending to Commodore Preble and to the Secretary of the Navy. Although the epistle is entirely personal in its character, it is well worth while to give it place here, and thus it appears, a true and authentic copy:

TRIPOLI, *November* 1, 1803.

MY DEAR SUSAN: With feelings of distress which I can not describe, I have to inform you that I have lost the beautiful frigate which was placed under my command by running her afoul of rocks, a few miles to the east of this harbor, which are not marked on the charts. After defending her as long as a ray of hope remained, I was obliged to surrender, and am now, with my officers and crew, confined in a prison in this place. I inclose to you a copy of my official letter to the Secretary of the Navy, from which you will learn all the circumstances in detail connected with our capture.

My anxiety and affliction does not arise from my confinement and deprivations in prison—these, indeed, I could bear if ten times more severe—but is caused by my absence, which may be a protracted one, from my dearly beloved Susan, and an apprehension, which constantly haunts me, that I may be censured by my countrymen. These impressions, which are seldom absent from my mind, act as a corroding canker at my heart. So maddened am I sometimes by the workings of my imagination that I can not refrain from exclaiming that it would have been a merciful dispensation of Providence if my head had been shot off by the enemy while our vessel lay rolling on the rocks.

You now see, my beloved wife, the cause of my distress. My situation in prison is entirely supportable; I have found here kind and generous friends, such as I hope the virtuous will meet in all situations; but if my professional character be blotched; if an attempt be made to taint my honor; if I am censured; if it does not kill me—it will at least deprive me of the power of looking any of my race in the face, always excepting, however, my young, kind, and sympathizing wife. If the world desert me, I am sure to find a welcome in her affection—to receive the support and condolence which none others can give.

I can not tell why I am so oppressed with apprehension. I am sure I acted according to my best judgment. My officers tell me that my conduct was faultless, that no one, indeed, could have done better; but this I attribute (perhaps in my weakness) to a generous wish on their part to sustain me in my affliction.

I hope soon to hear that your health is good, and that you, although grieved at my misfortune, are yet surrounded by dear and condoling friends, who will in some measure assuage your affliction. Perhaps, too, you will be able to tell me that I have done injustice to my countrymen—that so far from censuring, they sympathize, and some even applaud me. God grant that this may be the case—why should it not? The Americans are generous as they are brave. I must stop, my dear wife, for I see I am disclosing my weakness; these are the mere reveries which daily pass through my heated brain.

I beg you will not suppose our imprisonment is attended with suffering; on the contrary, it is, as I have already assured you, quite a supportable state. Your ever faithful and affectionate husband,

WILLIAM BAINBRIDGE.

Through the influence of Mr. Nissen, Bainbridge succeeded in getting all of his letters on board an out-bound vessel, and also sent a long communication addressed to Commodore Preble.

Bainbridge had stated his position rightly when he said that his stay in captivity promised not to be so much of a hardship as might be expected; Mr. Nissen had brought bedding, furniture, and all sorts of useful household articles to the place where the officers were confined, and he also brought word that the crew were in prison in a well-ventilated quarter of the castle. Said he, in referring to the Tripolitans:

"Although these people live by piracy, and have little or no legitimate trade, those high in authority have had intercourse with Christian and civilized nations, and have

Port of Tripoli.

dropped many of the attributes of the barbarian. Sidi Mohammed D'Ghiers is a man of fine character and sterling worth. You can trust in him implicitly."

Before a week had gone by time bore most heavily upon the hands of the captured officers; but one day

Nissen was announced, and looking out past their garden entrance, the officers saw that a donkey, with two large crates strapped on his back, was evidently waiting there to be unloaded. What was the delight of all hands when they ascertained that the load was nothing less than all of their books and a great deal of personal property which the Danish consul had purchased for a small sum at a sale of plunder taken from the Philadelphia. He was hailed with cheers, and, although he at first demurred, he was at once reimbursed for his expenditure.

When Bainbridge and he found a chance to speak together alone, the following conversation took place:

"Of course it is to be expected," began Mr. Nissen, "that any correspondence carried on between you and Commodore Preble will be *viséd* by the Tripolitan minister. I remember hearing a long time ago, when I was in France, a very interesting thing. You know a writing fluid may be prepared which is entirely invisible until the paper has been subjected to heat. The recipe for making this fluid, if I remember rightly, is something like this; in fact, I am quite sure this is correct."

With that he detailed a simple formula which Bainbridge copied, and put it to good use afterward, as will be proved.

It must not be thought that any degree of authority or discipline had been lost because of the fact that the life and routine of shipboard had been exchanged for the monotony of prison existence. The same discipline and respect was maintained, and, as soon as the books had arrived, the midshipmen resumed their studies under the direction of the officers. Classes in French and Spanish, history, navigation, and mathematics went on as they had on board ship. It was rather a remarkable fact that the majority of all those living together at the American consul's house were extremely young men, but one of the officers being above thirty years of age. The midshipmen, with one or two exceptions, were hardly more than boys. But the principles of honor and high sense of duty which they imbibed by contact with these young men, their leaders, counted for more than the habits of study which were rigidly enforced.

On the tenth day, while Bainbridge was exercising in the little courtyard surrounded by the high white wall, a messenger appeared with orders from the Bashaw for him to appear at once at the vice-regal palace, in order to talk with the regent upon a matter of vital interest. The Bashaw was a man very different in character and personality from Sidi Mohammed. He was evidently angry at something, for he scarcely waited for Bainbridge to be seated before beginning upon the subject.

"I have here," he said, "letters from the commander of one of my ships, the Messurre, complaining most bitterly of the treatment he has received from your Captain Chauncey, of the frigate John Adams. We have treated you kindly; we have given you of the best of the land, in order to prove that we are different from what we are held to be in the opinions of European nations. But this can not be forgotten. Any ill treatment of my subjects shall be retaliated upon the heads of you and your officers."

Bainbridge did not reply, for he saw that this was not all of the interview, and he knew that there was some reason other than this for his having been ordered to be present. There was to be a condition.

"If," continued the Bashaw, "you will write at once, before that shadow yonder has reached that spot near my hand, a letter to your Commodore Preble, asking him to release the prisoners from Tripoli, I will allow you to stay in your present place of confinement. If you do not, it will go hard with you. What have you to say?"

"Only this," Bainbridge replied: "I can not believe that the information you received is correct. It is the practice of Americans to treat prisoners with kindness and magnanimity and never with cruelty. In regard to the subjects of your Royal Highness, when our squadron lay in the Bay of Gibraltar I saw with my own eyes one of your captains visiting on familiar terms the officers of the various ships in company with the officers of the vessel in which he was supposed to be confined."

"You will not, then, write the letter?" asked the Bashaw threateningly.

"I can not write what you demand, for the reason that Commodore Preble is my senior," answered Bainbridge; "and besides this, my advice is useless, because by becoming your prisoner I have lost my rank and power."

"Have you any objections to stating the substance of our conversation in a report to the commander of the squadron?"

"None in the least," Bainbridge answered. And taking up pen and paper, he wrote for a few minutes and read aloud what he had written. This ended the meeting, and under guard he was sent back to join the officers, who were anxiously waiting to hear what had resulted.

In regard to what the Bashaw intended to do, Bainbridge could say nothing; but they were not long kept in ignorance, for within the hour a commotion was heard in front of the little building, a door to which had only been guarded by three armed men, two on the doorstep and one at the gate leading into the courtyard; but now one of the midshipmen came running down the stairway and knocked on the door of the room in which the officers were holding their conference. Porter arose hastily and opened it.

"The courtyard is full of soldiers heavily armed and bearing torches," said the middy.

"Surely they can not intend to turn us out at such short notice," grumbled Lieutenant Hunt.

"I suspect strongly, gentlemen," put in Bainbridge, "that such is their intention. At all events, the Bashaw has decided that we have been altogether too comfortable, and now intends to move us."

A noise in the hallway brought every one to his feet. The heavy door was unlocked, and a number of Tripolitan officers were seen standing there in consultation. Beyond them the startled Americans could see the courtyard filled with the swarthy-faced soldiery, and against the blackness of the night the torches flickered weirdly. Towering shadows wavered to and fro on the walls of the courtyard.

"What is the meaning of this?" Bainbridge inquired.

"We had come," answered the officer, "to escort you and your companions to a different place of confinement; but we have just received another order countermanding the first, and stating that your quarters will not be moved until to-morrow morning at nine o'clock, so I bid you prepare for departure."

Plainly this last message had been delivered just in time to prevent the discomfort of a hasty change of base. As it turned out afterward, it was the result of the intercession of Sidi Mohammed D'Ghies, who objected bravely to the Bashaw's sudden determination.

By nine o'clock the next morning the courtyard was again filled with soldiers under the command of the same officer who had reported the night before; but the prisoners were ready, each with his belongings done up in a bag or basket, and it was with a great deal of sorrow that they bade farewell to their comfortable quarters and set out through the narrow, dirty streets, bound for what they knew not.

They were not taken on the most direct route, but marched and countermarched through the lower portion of the town, much to the delight of the crowds through which their guards had difficulty in forcing their way. At last their prison dawned in sight—a low whitewashed building made of heavy stones and mortar, a filthy place that had been used by generations for smoking hides and for confining refractory or runaway slaves.

The officers were crowded into three rooms on the north side of the courtyard that had small grated windows opening on the well-guarded sea wall. On the opposite side of the open space were the large cells in which the crew of the Philadelphia were imprisoned. The brave lads, when they saw that their officers had come to join them, broke out into a cheer as the party marched through the yard.

The quarters that Bainbridge and the rest found unprepared for them possessed no accommodations fit to make life bearable. The heavy doors were shut upon them and they sat down upon the damp stone floor. Hours went by. No one came to see them. Not a drop of water nor a bit of food had passed their lips. About five o'clock in the afternoon they managed to communicate their distress to the crew confined across the way, and the loyal Jack tars bribed one of their own keepers to bring over a portion of their scant evening meal—black bread and water with a small cruse of olive oil, which was the food of the lower order of Algerine slaves and laborers.

Before it was dusk there came a clanging at the door, bolts from the outside were dropped, and a strange-looking figure entered. It was a man clad in the loose-flowing garments of the Tripolitan sailor, with turban and turned-up slippers, but his face had none of the darkness of skin; it was red and mottled, and the chin was overgrown with a thin beard of wiry red. His first words created more of a sensation than did his remarkable appearance.

"Weel, weel, and here's where ye are noo! Is Captain Bainbridge here?"

"I am Captain Bainbridge," said a voice from the corner; "and may I ask whom I have the honor of addressing?"

"Admiral Lisle, of the Tripolitan navy, is my name. Hoot, mon, but this is nae place for the confinement of officers and gentlemen!"

"We are not here by our own choice," answered Bainbridge, "and we are very willing to exchange it for anything better, for in fact we could not be treated to a worse fate than be left here where we are."

"It may be summat of your ain fault," the odd-looking admiral replied, winking his little Scotch eyes knowingly.

"May I ask you to explain yourself, sir?"

"Wha don't you accede to the wishes of the Bashaw? 'Tis naught he demands but a little scribbling on a bit of paper that will do ye no harm to write for him. You're daft, mon, not to do it."

"You'll pardon me," interposed Bainbridge. "I have not the least idea how great is your knowledge upon the subject of which you speak; but mark you this: the Bashaw can torture me; he can lop off my head; but there is one thing that he can not do: he can not force me to commit an act that is incompatible with the honor of an American officer. If this is the object of your visit to us, I can only say that you will obtain neither satisfaction nor promises. If it is an answer you demand, you have it."

The "admiral" appeared to be somewhat confused at

the force with which Bainbridge had uttered the last words, and he mumbled something inarticulate as he backed out of the doorway. No sooner had he disappeared than Porter, Jones, and Hunt grasped Bainbridge's hand in turn. Without a word he understood that these men felt as he did; no explanation was necessary and none was offered.

Darkness came on. Just before midnight the door to their prison was again opened, and there stood the same guard that had escorted them thither in the morning.

"Follow us," said one of the officers. And forming a column of twos, the prisoners marched out into the night, taking their dunnage with them.

This time they were not marched through the by-streets, and in less than a quarter of an hour they found themselves back once more at the house that had belonged to the American consul before the outbreak of hostilities. Now Bainbridge, to his delight, found that his first missive had reached Commodore Preble, for in charge of Mr. Nissen an answer was received, and, by means of the sympathetic ink, communication was established, the Danish consul sending the epistle to his *confrère* at Malta, and by this latter gentleman they were forwarded to the commander of the American squadron.

It had been found necessary to resort to this means, as the Bashaw subjected all communications to a rigid inspection and kept copies of all the correspondence.

A month went by. School was resumed, but the confinement was beginning to tell upon the spirits of the officers, although they were well fed and comfortably housed.

With the crew who were in the same loathsome dungeon that they had been at first thrown into, affairs were going very hard indeed. They were not used to the food, and sickness had begun among them. Bainbridge and his officers had not been permitted to hold intercourse with them, and knew nothing of their condition, only having been informed that they were kept employed at their trades if they had any—those who possessed none working upon the fortifications.

From an upper window of their house, which was near the water front, a glimpse of the harbor could be obtained; and occasionally the captain or one of his lieutenants had been allowed to stroll along the ramparts in charge of a small guard. Bainbridge had looked many times with deep sorrow at the Philadelphia, his fine old ship, as she lay there well protected by the guns of the castle, herself a great adjunct to the protection of the town, for her guns had been fished up and replaced on her decks. He regretted more than once that he had not proceeded to extreme measures and, instead of scuttling her, set her on fire when he had seen that her defense was useless.

He returned from one of these walks that he had taken on the 5th of December, elated with an idea that had entered his mind. It was one that would require immediate co-operation of Preble and the squadron, and demanded great intrepidity and daring for its successful accomplishment; but brave and adventurous spirits he knew were not lacking. He could have called the names of a half dozen young men now with the commodore to whom he would intrust the leadership.

He had noticed that all of the enemy's gunboats were hauled up on shore, and that, owing to the transfer of guns, the small crescent-shaped battery was almost in a dismantled condition. Dipping his pen into the invisible ink, he wrote the following letter, sending it to Preble through the usual channels. It does not detract from the glory of any one subsequently connected with the undertaking to publish this epistle; it merely places the honor of originating the plan where it assuredly belongs. Writes Bainbridge under date of the 5th:

"Charter a small merchant schooner, fill her with men, and have her commanded by fearless and determined officers. Let the vessel enter the harbor at night, with her men secreted below decks. Steer her directly on board the frigate, and then the officers and men board, sword in hand, and there is not a doubt of their success and without very heavy loss. It would be necessary to take several good rowboats in order to facilitate the retreat after the enterprise had been accomplished. The frigate in her present condition is a powerful auxiliary battery for the defense of the harbor. Though it will be impossible to remove her from her anchorage, and thus restore this beautiful vessel to our navy, yet, as she may, and no doubt will be repaired, an important end will be gained by her destruction."

Upon receiving this communication Commodore Preble called a council of his officers, and by the earliest opportunity he wrote an answer to Captain Bainbridge informing him that preparations were being made to carry out the plans as he suggested, and that his friend, Lieutenant Stephen Decatur, had volunteered to command the expedition.

Time went on and yet nothing was done. The winter passed and a new year began. Various schemes were proposed for the destruction of Tripoli, Bainbridge stating in a letter to Preble that he thought the landing of four or five thousand troops would result in the taking of the town. But affairs looked very dark. Hearing of the condition of the crew, Bainbridge petitioned the Bashaw to allow him to do something to help to make their life more bearable, and again, through the kind offices of Sidi Mohammed Dgheis, clothing and more sustaining food were allowed to be sent in to them from the American squadron.

Mr. Nissen continued to lend his assistance, and thus cemented the friendship that had begun during the early days of captivity.

CHAPTER XIV.

The Mohammedans are a peculiarly religious people. They observe the festivals of their sect with the greatest care and faithfulness, and it happens that once a year there comes a period of thirty days which is known as the feast of Ramadan. It is a period of religious abstinence, during which the good Mohammedan imposes upon himself moral and physical restraint to an extreme degree. He is compelled by his creed to kindly thoughts and deeds, such as hospitality to strangers and charity to bitterest enemies.

During the day little or no food is partaken of between sunrise and sunset; but in the night season, it may be remarked, they make up for a great deal of lost time. At the end of this month of daily fasting and nightly feasting there comes the Biarian festival, which amounts to a period of gorging and rejoicing covering from three to six days.

From the lowest household in its mud-wall hut to the Bashaw in his palace all hands turn to and enjoy themselves.

On this occasion Bainbridge and Lieutenant Porter were invited to the Bashaw's residence, where they were treated as guests of honor and received with Eastern civilities. They also attended a feast of the Prime Minister, who was a Russian by birth, although he had lived for a long time in Tripoli. The largest ceremony they attended, however, and one that exceeded in point of splendor all the others, was a dinner, or better, banquet, at the residence of their good friend Sidi Mohammed D'Ghiers, Minister of State. Through his intercession also, permission had been obtained for the officers under a small guard, and on their parole of honor, to ride a few miles back into the country. It was a great relief to them to secure these outings, but it made their confinement perhaps the harder to bear. Yet what they were then undergoing was nothing compared to that held in store for them.

One day in the early part of the month Porter and Lieutenant Hunt, astride of two small mules, had ridden out beyond the walls of the city. Two armed janizaries accompanied them, but kept at a respectful distance. It was a fine warm morning, and a breeze that blew from the north rustled the branches of the trees. It was a beautiful sight. On all sides were the barley and wheat fields, with their waving grain; the groves of dates, of olive and of fig trees; the orchards of lemon, orange, apricot, and peach; the well-kept gardens that surrounded the country houses of the wealthy. They could scarcely imagine themselves prisoners, although they knew at any time they might exchange all this for close confinement and blank dungeon walls.

All at once they turned about a corner of a lane, and there, at about a half mile's distance, they could see the blue waters of the Mediterranean. The officers had no idea that they had been so close to the sea, and they halted a minute to observe the beautiful effect made by this vivid patch of blue inclosed by the green frame of the arching trees.

"It is almost enough to incline one to turn Turk and settle down here forever," said Lieutenant Hunt with a sigh.

"Well, it appears that we shall most probably stay

here for some time to come," answered Porter. "Not a movement yet from our fleet, and Preble is not a man to hesitate or to put off action. In my opinion something will be done soon that will relieve us from our position of uncertainty at least."

"Well, I'd like to know where he is and what he's doing," Hunt remarked, loosening his long legs from the stirrups. "This is all very fine, but I'd just like to know. You see—— By jove!" he exclaimed, suddenly interrupting himself, "look down there, man, straight ahead."

Porter followed his glance. In the little space inclosed by the green frame was a fine, large ship, with all sails spread, sailing to the westward. She was less than two miles from shore.

"The Constitution!" exclaimed Porter. "I know her by her lofty rig."

"Ay, and here comes another," interposed Hunt. "The Nautilus, I take it."

Yes, there they were, three or four now, seen all at once, and on they came until they had passed by.

When the officers arrived that evening at the little house with the heavily barred windows they had a story to tell.

Preble was in the offing! And the next day this was confirmed, for Nissen called to see them and brought them word. But nothing out of the ordinary occurred. What was Preble doing?

On the 15th of February, about midnight, Bainbridge awakened with a start. There was no mistake, that was the sound of a heavy cannon! Then another boom, and a distant rattle of musketry and a roar of firing arose from the direction of the harbor.

From the little window upstairs in the room where the midshipmen slept a glimpse of the waters inside the mole could be obtained, and it happened by luck that very often as she swung at her anchor the captured frigate occupied this very space, a tantalizing sight to the eyes of the prisoners.

Bainbridge had hardly reached the door when he heard a shrill, boyish cheer from the "steerage," as the middys called their dormitory.

"The Philadelphia is on fire! The Philadelphia is on fire!" cried young Reefer Biddle, who, in scanty attire, was leaning over the stairway.

Way was made for the officers at the window, and soon Bainbridge was standing there observing with great satis-

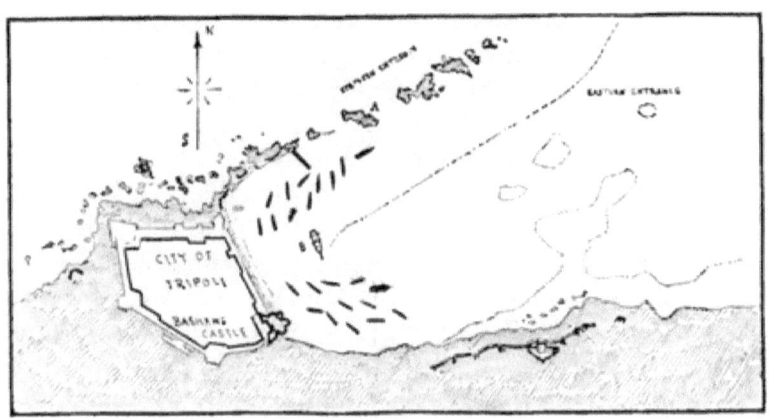

The harbor of Tripoli.
B, position of the Philadelphia; the dotted line shows the course of the boarding vessel.

faction the red glare, growing and growing, until he could make out the outlines of his vessel and see the flames pouring from her ports. She was swinging at her cables, and gradually she worked around until the hull was hidden by the neighboring houses and nothing but the glare in the sky showed that she was blazing merrily.

Suddenly there came the roar of a tremendous explosion. Bright flying sparks like rockets were hurled into the air, and when they had fallen the glare had disappeared.

"The end!" said Bainbridge calmly, turning to the officers. "Who do you suppose did that?"

He knew himself, of course, but he wished to see what they would say.

"Stephen Decatur!" exclaimed a small midshipman involuntarily, clapping his fist to his mouth after he had spoken, as a bashful schoolgirl might.

"Perhaps it was Somers," ventured one of the lieutenants.

"Mr. Gamble was right," remarked Bainbridge; "it was Stephen Decatur, unless I am much mistaken, and God help and save him and all the brave men who assisted him."

"Amen!" said the rest in chorus.

This is not the place to tell of this successful expedition, for it belongs to another story; but the fact remains that Stephen Decatur, accompanied by Lieutenants James Lawrence, Joseph Bainbridge, Midshipman Charles Morris, and seventy fine seamen, had carried out Bainbridge's plan to the letter. They had sailed in in a large ketch, and had warped themselves alongside the Philadelphia. They boarded her, cutlas in hand, and set fire to her, and escaped without the loss of a single man and with but four of their number wounded!

The next morning Nissen hastened to see his friends. Although he could not but reflect their elation that was so evident, his face was clouded with a look of worry.

"The Bashaw's in a frightful rage," said he, "and will wreak his vengeance somewhere. I fear that he will vent it upon you. He would not have lost that ship for anything in the kingdom. I trust, my dear friends, that

you will not suffer. I am going to see Sidi Mohammed to-day and find out how affairs now stand."

No notice was apparently taken of the action, however, except that the presents of fruit and fresh eatables now suddenly ceased, and affairs went on much as usual until there came a most momentous day, the 1st of March, two weeks after the destruction of the frigate.

Then, without warning, the officers were informed that they were about to be moved to another prison, and by twelve o'clock they had begun the uncomfortable march through the crowded streets of the town. The Bashaw had at last found a place to his liking in which to incarcerate them. It was a horribly damp and cold apartment, whose only aperture was a small window well above the height of a man's head and grated with strong iron bars. It was to be their home for fourteen weary months. They were even denied the privilege that the crew of the Philadelphia were given—that of exercise in the open air—for the Bashaw was employing the prisoners upon the works and fortifications that he was pushing to a close.

Of course plans for escaping from their prison were indulged in almost without end. Nissen succeeded, with a great deal of difficulty, in gaining access to them, and smuggled out a letter destined for the squadron then cruising off the mouth of the harbor, for the blockade of the port was now rigidly enforced.

All regular communication between the prisoners and the outside world was interdicted by the Bashaw's orders; but the letter to Commodore Preble proposed that he should send into the harbor on a certain night five fast rowing boats, if (and it was a very big " if " indeed) the prisoners should succeed in digging their way under the castle to the bottom of the sea wall. The tunnel was begun, but before it progressed very far it was found that the entrance of it would be beneath the surface of the water, and the idea had to be abandoned.

Sentinels had been placed along the sea wall and the shore for several miles on either side of the city, and it would have been impossible for boats to have rowed into the harbor without being observed and subjected to a destructive fire.

One dreary night, as Bainbridge and Porter and Lieutenants Hunt and Smith lay talking together in low whispers, Lieutenant Jones crawled over to them.

"I've been thinking, gentlemen," he observed, making his way into the center of the group, "that it might be possible to explore the adjoining apartment here on our port hand. We may find a window unbarred, or some way by which we can reach the sea wall, and lower ourselves to the ramparts."

"It will do no harm at least to try," said Bainbridge, knowing that it would give employment if nothing else, and keep their minds from dwelling upon their unfortunate situation. So the next day the prisoners were told off into watches, and systematic work was begun.

With the aid of some hoop iron and one knife, the mortar was removed from several large stones in the side of the room; but every day it had to be replaced, or at least made to appear all right when their prison was inspected. Behind the stones they found that the space had been filled in with earth, loosely mixed with mortar, and all this had to be removed carefully in order to hide traces of their work. At last, however, there was nothing to be done but thrust out a few bricks on the opposite side to make an entrance into the neighboring apartment. By careful listening they had determined that it was unoccupied. One moonlight night the stones were removed, and by means of a few well-directed kicks a hole was made large enough for a man to work his body through.

Bainbridge and two of the lieutenants made the first reconnoissance. It was a large open space in the extreme wing of the prison. The roof had partly fallen in, and way above their heads was a small window. Standing upon the shoulders of Lieutenant Porter, Jones managed to work his way up to it. As soon as he reached the grating he uttered an exclamation of delight; the bars were loose, and with a little manipulation he declared that they would fetch away. The window looked down upon the top of the rampart at an angle where a few heavy guns pointed out over the harbor, but it was a drop of forty feet to the water's edge, and fully fifteen from the window to the ground outside.

As nothing could be done that night, they again returned to their companions and blocked up the passageway.

Now the following plan was formed: A long rope was plaited out of their blankets, and it was arranged that the strongest swimmers should make their way into the next room, climb to the window, descend to the ramparts, and lower themselves down to the water's edge. Once there, they were to swim off to a small boat that was anchored about a quarter of a mile from shore, take possession of her, and trust to luck to escape to the squadron.

The scheme necessitated leaving some of their number behind. Bainbridge was not a good swimmer, and although Hunt and Jones promised to take care of him in the water, he determined to remain and share the fate of the unfortunates.

One dark night silent farewells were taken, and a party of twelve, dressed only in their shirts and trousers, in order the better to facilitate their movements, crawled through the aperture. In less than an hour a scratching was heard upon the opposite wall; the stones were again withdrawn, and they filed back again. They reported that everything had gone well until the very last minute, when, just as they were about making the line fast to one of the guns in order that they might lower themselves to the water, the relief of the guard approached and they had to give up the plan.

It was a fortunate thing that they had been forced to return, as the vessel to which they had intended swimming, had changed her anchorage, and all might have been drowned or shot by the sentries if they had attempted to land.

This was only one of numerous and repeated failures. Upon one occasion they had undermined the rampart and entered a large vault, but in doing so they had weakened the supports so that the whole affair caved in beneath the weight of a heavy cannon, a forty-two pounder, that had been resting above it. The prisoners were now suffering from the foul and stagnant air, and were growing pale and weak. Many times had they begged and implored for better ventilation, but, receiving no attention, they determined boldly to make it for themselves, and to this end opened a large hole plain to the view, admitting the fresh air from the outside. When their jailer, a bad-tempered black man of the desert named Sossey, discovered this, he waxed exceeding angry, and threatened them with terrible punishment, asking at the same time who had " dared to do this act."

Porter stepped forward and informed the jailer that he was the guilty one. Immediately he was hurried away from his companions and placed in solitary confinement in a horrible dungeon not more than eight feet square. On the second day he was brought before Sidi Mohammed, who expressed his sorrow that he could do nothing to help the prisoners, as the Bashaw was implacable. But, nevertheless, Porter was returned to his companions and Sossey was removed from his position.

But the failing spirits of all were revived when, on the 12th of July, almost at daybreak, a furious cannonading was heard from the northward toward the mouth of the harbor.

CHAPTER XV.

"Preble is at it again. Hurrah!" exclaimed Porter with a laugh. "Oh, I wish we were there with him!"

He dashed his heavy hat angrily down on the floor of the cell.

"Come, let us go into the next room through our passageway," suggested Jones. "We can watch what's going on."

No sooner had he spoken than a heavy explosion sounded quite near to them.

"Hurrah!" cried Bainbridge. "Gentlemen, that was a good Yankee shell."

Another one burst in the direction of the Bashaw's palace.

"I'll bet their high-cockolorum bowed his old head to that," said a middy.

By this time the stones were removed, and as many as could crowd through into the next room did so, and soon the grated window and the aperture was filled with excited faces.

"Just look at those three boats bear down on that division of the enemy—nine of them, by George! I'll wager that we'll see some tall fighting now," cried Jones.

It was so far off that the boats looked to be mere dots. But the white smoke soon blotted out even the details, and the firing became steady. When the breeze had cleared the air a little it was seen that three of the Tripolitan gunboats had been taken and the others were in flight, making their way with plashing sweeps up the harbor. One of the big gunboats was some lengths behind the rest.

"Look there! Look there!" cried Jones, pointing. "See that small boat chasing the whole lot of them."

"It's one of their own," suggested Smith.

"You're mistaken, sir," said Bainbridge quietly, for his eyes were like those of a hawk. "That's one of the ship's cutters, and they're some of our lads putting their backs into that steady stroke."

"They're after that last galley, then," roared Porter, "and they are going to catch her, too! I'll bet Decatur is in that cutter!"

Just as he spoke the men at the oars tossed them inboard, and almost to a man they leaped for the side of the Tripolitan. The other five sail continued on their way and did not stop to help their companion. Soon the latter was observed to come about into the wind and, with the cutter in tow, make for the American line. She had been taken in five minutes!

One of the Yankee gunboats had grounded near the crescent-shaped battery, where she was subjected to a terrible fire; but she managed to get off, replying pluckily the while with her one big gun.

"Hurrah for the man who commands that little skipjack!" shouted Lieutenant Hunt.

"Cleverly done, indeed!" Bainbridge exclaimed, rubbing his hands together with delight. "Did you mark, gentlemen, how he crept out of range of that big gun on the point without receiving his fire? He is brave and clever."

The captain did not know that it was his own brother, Lieutenant Joseph Bainbridge, whom he was eulogizing; nor did he know until a long time afterward that the little boat that had captured the lagging Tripolitan was commanded by Stephen Decatur, and that it was to revenge the death, or better, the murder of his own brother, by the corsair who held command, that had tempted him to set out in pursuit to seek revenge, for the Tripolitan had surrendered before and had then risen like a dastard and annihilated the boarding party led by James Decatur. He paid the penalty a few minutes later. But all the story of the heroic deeds of those of the fleet has been told elsewhere. This is but a chronicle of the doings of Bainbridge and his fellow prisoners. Yet we must relate what they saw that day.

Off to one side a separate little action was taking place. One American gunboat was fighting five of the enemy at pistol-shot range. This was the gallant Somers, the man who would never know defeat, and a cheer went up from the anxious watchers within the prison walls, as they saw all five of the corsairs make haste to join in the retreat. The Yankee boats pursued and the Tripolitans rallied in force, and it appeared that the few American sail were in great jeopardy, for they were almost surrounded. But straight into the mouth of the harbor sailed the great frigate Constitution to the rescue! On she came until well within the range of the guns of the battery; then her broadside spurted flame and smoke, and the retreat of the brave little American squadron was covered.

The Constitution came about within three cable lengths of the flanking fortress, and as she pointed her nose once more toward the entrance of the harbor, she silenced the guns with the discharge of her port battery, while with the starboard she sent shot and shell flying over the walls of the city in among the houses and the palace gardens.

The Bashaw had promised the people of the city rare sport if the American fleet should ever venture within

Watching the bombardment from the Tripoli prison cell.

the harbor mouth. He had been watching the action from one of his windows, but when the Constitution fired that last broadside he fled unceremoniously and hid in his bomb-proof cellar chamber.

Mr. Nissen was the only one of the foreign consuls who had stayed in town after the beginning of the bombardment, but he had become so devoted to the interests of his American friends that he remained at the risk of his life in order to be near them should his services be required. Several shells fell in and about his house, but fortunately none of them had exploded. It had pained the lookers on, who hoped that the attack might result in their release, to see the withdrawal of the squadron; but they recognized that nothing could be gained by venturing farther into the harbor, and the gallantry of their companions put them all in good spirits and gave them much to talk about for some time to come.

The result of this first action might be told in a few words: The three captured boats contained one hundred and three men, of whom forty-seven were killed and twenty-six wounded. Three of the enemy's vessels were sunk with all their crews, and a number of guns in the batteries along the shore had been dismounted.

On the fifth day of August Mr. Nissen brought the news that Preble had returned all the wounded Tripolitan prisoners, and Nissen himself had heard one of the captured officers say to the Prime Minister that the Americans in battle were fiercer than lions, yet in their treatment of prisoners they were even kinder than Mussulmen. The result of this humane treatment on the part of Commodore Preble was that the Bashaw, in thanking him, stated that if any injured Americans fell into his hands he would treat them with equal kindness.

Some negotiations in regard to the establishment of peace were now begun, but they were soon discontinued owing to the extravagant demands of the Bashaw, who was yet very proud and haughty.

A second attack upon the city followed, and much injury was done by round shot and shell. Most unfortunately, a small American vessel was blown up by a red-hot shot, losing ten of her crew killed and six wounded.

On the 27th of August a third attack was begun, and an incident that occurred came very near ending Bainbridge's career on earth. He had been unwell for some two or three days and was lying on his pallet of straw, when the rest of the officers hurried to the points of vantage to watch the bombardment that had just begun. The Constitution had opened fire at long range, and it was by one of her shots that Bainbridge nearly lost his life. A thirty-two pound cannon ball struck squarely on the outside of the wall, almost above his head. The masonry gave way under the impact, and the captain was literally covered with almost a ton of stone and mortar. His officers, who were at the end of the narrow cell, hastened to him and extricated him at once. It was found that his ankle had been badly crushed by the falling of a part of the embattlement, and he was covered with cuts and bruises.

So hot had become the fire of the American squadron that the Tripolitan guards fled from their places on the terrace ramparts and hid behind the walls of the prison. Their cowardice excited the merriment of the Yankee midshipmen, and they were jeered unmercifully. Angry at this, the poltroons threw stones in at the prisoners through the windows that opened upon the yard. The midshipmen armed themselves with bits of the *débris* scattered about their apartment and returned the fire, a most riotous proceeding in the eyes of the head jailer, for he threatened to shoot down the offenders if they did not desist. This stopped the miniature battle; but Bainbridge wrote a note to Sidi Mohammed, complaining that the guards had been the first offenders, and he had the satisfaction of being informed that the villain who began all the trouble had been severely bastinadoed and dismissed.

A few days later news was brought that the squadron was again entering the harbor, and soon the guns of the forts encircling the shore had begun to roar defiance.

The enemy's galleys did not make much of a fight upon this occasion, and giving away, the American squadron pursued them within musket shot of the large fort on the east, the Tripolitan admiral congregating all of his fleet close under the walls. The Yankee squadron separated, and part of it sailed boldly in upon the mass of Tripolitan shipping, while the rest bravely engaged the forts. Two bomb ketches kept on until quite close to shore and began throwing shells into the town with great effect. But from their exposed position it was seen that they had no chance to survive the furious fire directed at them. They both seemed doomed, when all at once Preble, in the Constitution, came down as he had done before to help them out. So close was he to the terraces that the figures of the men upon the spar deck could be distinguished. Seventy guns were playing down upon him, but so rapidly and effectually did the Yankees serve their broadsides that the Tripolitans slackened their fire, and under cover of the frigate the bomb ketches retreated safely.

This time the Bashaw had received a severe fright. He had lost two more of his fleet, and suffered a great deal of damage by the shells that fell in the heart of the city. But, although the Americans had been subjected to a criss-cross fire, not a man was killed in the whole affair, and the damage to the squadron consisted mainly of wrecked spars and injured rigging.

Under the orders of the Scotch-Turkish admiral it was concluded not to use the galleys except as an assistant force to the land batteries, and they remained moored stem and stern in a compact mass at the upper bend of

A brass cannon captured from the Tripolitans, now at Annapolis.

the harbor. Nothing could tempt them from their safe retreat.

No other demonstration was made by the squadron during the following week, and despair and gloom settled upon the little band confined behind the gray stone walls, for it became apparent that the small fleet in the offing could effect little or nothing against the powerful batteries, although they might destroy considerable property in the city itself.

A long period of captivity stared them in the face. They could see no end to it, and it was no easy matter to stir up the courage of the sick and despairing.

Between nine and ten o'clock on the evening of the 4th of September, while they were preparing themselves to pass through the long hot night, there came a terrific explosion that jarred the air and sent particles of plaster falling in all directions. A little midshipman, awakened from his sleep, cried aloud in fright. The report had been preceded by a red flash, as if a great thunderbolt had exploded just outside their grated window.

"What do you suppose that was," exclaimed Jones, starting up and rushing to the small ventilating window that, owing to the kindness of their friend Sidi, had not been filled in.

Every one had crowded about him, but there was nothing to be seen except the darkness of the night.

"Stop talking! Listen!" ordered Bainbridge.

From the direction of the harbor came cries and distant murmurings. A long wail, like a chorus of many voices, rose in the air and died away; then all was silence.

"A magazine has exploded," said Porter.

"It sounded to me," replied Jones, "as if it came from out on the bay."

In the morning they all learned what it meant. That explosion sounded the death knell of the gallant young Somers, the popular and well-beloved young officer who was known to all of them. Lieutenant Wadsworth, Midshipman Israel, and ten brave seamen shared his fate. And with them over two hundred Tripolitans lost their lives. Every reader of American history is familiar with the story of how Somers sailed in in the ketch Intrepid, laden with one hundred barrels of gunpowder, for the purpose of destroying the Tripolitan vessels huddled within the mole; how she had been boarded just before she reached her destination, and the terrible result of the explosion. In what manner the trains of powder had been ignited has never been found out. It may have been from accident, or it may have been done in a moment of desperation by the heroic Somers himself.

Two days later Bainbridge and his four lieutenants were permitted to view the bodies that had washed ashore. So mutilated and disfigured were they by the explosion that it was impossible to identify any of them. But over their graves Bainbridge read a funeral service, and they were placed to rest with all the small honors that could be given them.

All of these attacks made the Bashaw more inclined to

negotiation for peace, but yet his demands were considered exorbitant, and the United States sent out a larger squadron, under the command of Commodore Barron, who superseded Preble, the latter returning to America, leaving the Constitution under the command of his young friend, Stephen Decatur. The new commodore retired with his ships to Syracuse, and began making plans for active operations in the spring. It was now decided to attempt the reduction of Tripoli by means of a land force, acting in conjunction with the deposed ruler of the country, for the Bashaw then upon the throne had usurped the power that rightfully belonged to his uncle. But this is a separate story. Not hearing from Barron, and receiving no news from their country for a long time, the unhappy prisoners deemed themselves deserted, and indulged in the most desperate plans and projects for escape, one of which was to break jail and storm the castle of the Bashaw. But, owing to the watchfulness of the guards, nothing was accomplished, and black despair settled down upon them.

CHAPTER XVI.

At last word was brought again through Mr. Nissen that General Eaton, an officer of the American army, had joined forces with those of the deposed Bashaw's, and that they were marching through the deserts of Libya, with the intention of taking Tripoli in the rear. The Tripolitan potentate displayed great consternation at hearing this, and redoubled his efforts to increase the fortifications in and about the city. But one fine morning the American squadron appeared off the harbor, and glorious indeed was the sight of the flag.

Negotiations now began in earnest, and the Bashaw appointed the Spanish consul to represent him in a conference held on board the frigate Constitution. When Bainbridge heard who had been chosen he became most anxious to apprise Commodore Barron, Rodgers, and Colonel Lear, United States Consul General to the Barbary powers, of the Spaniards' enmity toward the United States. Sidi Mohammed, the wise and far-seeing, also doubted the good will of the Bashaw's emissary, and was most anxious to come to some terms of settlement.

The result of a conference held in the prison was that Bainbridge himself should solicit permission to pay a visit to the squadron under his parole of honor to return, and that his companions would pledge their lives for the carrying out of the promise. Porter was appointed spokesman, and with the assistance of Mr. Nissen he obtained an interview with Sidi Mohammed. The Minister of State agreed that the plan was a good one, but doubted whether the Bashaw would consent to placing such trust in any one. As for himself, he declared that he would exact no pledge from Bainbridge but his own word of honor. After some deliberation he agreed to ask the Bashaw to consider it, and to use his best offices in gaining a favorable answer to the request. Thinking it might be a good plan to have something to show, he asked that the officers would draw up and sign a paper in order that he might show it to his High Mightiness. It was also thought best for the captain to accompany him to represent his cause.

This Bainbridge agreed to, and he was witness to a remarkable scene. He had learned enough of the language to understand what was going forward, and his respect and admiration for Sidi Mohammed rose mightily, although he had always considered him most friendly.

"Are you so mad as to believe that Captain Bainbridge will return after getting on board a vessel of his own nation, simply because he has made a declaration to that effect?" asked the Bashaw with a sneer.

The minister made a low bow.

"You have the pledge of his officers," he answered.

"True enough," the Bashaw put in, "but I value Captain Bainbridge as a prisoner more than all of his officers put together, and I place no reliance on their pledge."

"Pray listen to me," answered the minister. "Your servant has lived long in Christian countries and has seen much of their officers, and he knows that the pledge of a parole of honor is not to be broken."

The Bashaw shrugged his shoulders.

"I have contracted a friendship for this American," went on Sidi Mohammed. "I have full confidence in his honor. You know that I am a Tripolitan by birth, that all my affections are for my country, and that I would propose no measure by which it would be injured. Grant Bainbridge's request, and I will leave my son in your castle, and in the event of his not returning according to my promise, you can take the head off him whose life I value more than my own."

Although the privilege was absolutely unprecedented, the Bashaw could not but yield to these circumstances. But no one about the court believed that the Christian would return, and they considered Sidi Mohammed a ruined man indeed.

On the first day of June, 1805, Bainbridge left the shelter of the castle in a small boat and was rowed off to the fleet. He spent the day in consultation with the officers, and returned late at night to the palace, where he waited upon Sidi Mohammed, who had not displayed the slightest anxiety, although the Bashaw had begun to rebuke him for inducing him to place the least reliance on the word of a "Christian dog." His surprise at seeing Bainbridge was ill-concealed. When he heard the terms upon which the United States was disposed to treat he became furiously angry and declined to enter into further negotiations, but the next day a special meeting was held, and in place of the Spaniard, Mr. Nissen, the Danish consul, was selected to renew the negotiations, and went on board the Constitution to confer with the American officers. Without trouble they came to an agreement upon which to form the basis of a treaty.

On the 3d of June the Bashaw stated that he was ready to listen to propositions and to consider whether peace should be rejected or concluded. Bainbridge and Mr. Nissen were invited to be present at the council. The meeting was held in the large trial chamber of the palace. The members of the Bashaw's cabinet and the invited guests and representatives sat about arranged in the form of a crescent, the regent being in the center, his Prime Minister being on the right, and the Minister for State and Foreign Affairs on the left hand. The strangers were invited to be seated, and the Bashaw turned to Captain Bainbridge.

"In order that everything shall be perfectly fair," he said, "the debates on the subject of this treaty are to be carried on in French, and if you, sir, understand the language, you will be able to hear the opinions of my ministers from their own mouths. In thus admitting you to my private divan you have received an honor never before conferred on a prisoner in Barbary."

Then arising with a great deal of dignity, he submitted the question of "peace or war with the United States." The various members of the council addressed the regent in turn in well-chosen words, in short but direct speeches. After the debate had continued to the end a vote was taken, and it was seen that of the eight who had the privilege of casting a ballot, only two were for peace—Sidi Mohammed D'Ghiers and the Rais of Marine. Each requested the privilege of adding a few more remarks, and with a great deal of eloquence they pressed their claim, with the result that two of the members came over to their side of the question upon a second voting. The Bashaw now arose.

"Four of you are for peace," he said, "and four for war. Which party shall I satisfy? How shall I act?"

He hesitated and resumed his seat as Sidi Mohammed stepped forward.

"You are our Prince and Master," the minister said, making obeisance. "You have not called us here to dictate to you, but to hear our opinions. It now remains for you to act as you please; but let me entreat you, for your own interests and the happiness of your people, to make it peace."

Again he bowed low and returned to his seat.

The Bashaw cast his eye about the half circle, and leaning forward, took a signet from the bosom of his silken gown and pressed it down upon the treaty.

" It is peace! " he said.

CHAPTER XVII.

It did not take long to ratify the treaty, and Mr. Nissen brought it on board the flagship, signed with the Bashaw's signature in due form.

Now it had been nineteen months and more since the day that Bainbridge and his officers had found themselves prisoners. On the morrow they would be free men. The news traveled quickly through the great prison where the crew were then confined. Cheer after cheer arose as the Tripolitan castle fired a salute of twenty-one guns, and from out in the harbor the Constitution answered it.

The terms arranged upon were, in short, as follows: There should be an exchange of prisoners " man for man so far as they would go; that the Bashaw should send all the Americans in his power on board the squadron off Tripoli; that his subjects should be brought over from Syracuse and delivered to him with all convenient speed; and as he had three hundred Americans, more or less, and the United States squadron one hundred Tripolitans, more or less, the American commissioners engaged to give for the balance in the Bashaw's favor $60,000; and that a treaty of peace should be made on honorable and mutually beneficial terms."

The crew were distributed, upon their release, among the various ships of the squadron, and, without loss of any time, all sail was made to the northward.

A jailer, a slave to the Tripolitans, had treated them so kindly that they had insisted upon purchasing his freedom, and they succeeded in so doing with the advance money from their wages to the amount of seven hundred dollars.

At Syracuse a court of inquiry was held on board the Constitution, and an investigation was made under orders of the Secretary of the Navy in regard to the loss of the Philadelphia. Bainbridge was acquitted immediately and with honor; and as soon as possible he returned to the United States, landing in Hampton, Va.

He was received with every mark of approbation by the public and by the officials at Washington, and as soon as Congress had been informed of the high conduct of the Danish consul they passed resolutions of thanks to him for his benevolent actions.

Although Bainbridge was appointed by the Secretary of the Navy to the command of the navy yard of New York, he found that his financial condition demanded attention; so, obtaining a furlough, he embarked once more in the merchant service, in which he passed two years. In 1808 he returned to the service and was appointed to the position left vacant by the death of his old friend Commodore Preble. But affairs looked very stormy, owing to the continued impressment of American seamen into the service of England. The Government at last concluded to order the best officers to active duty, and Bainbridge was relieved of the command of the Portland station and was ordered to repair on board the frigate President, then lying at Washington. There were many repairs to be made, however, before she was ready for sea, and it was not until July, 1809, that he started southward on a coastwise cruise.

As hostilities between our country and England were imminent, and in Bainbridge's mind unavoidable, no trouble was spared to make the crew of the frigate under his command able and effective. During a long and stormy winter he kept at sea, and when he returned in May of the next year no better drilled or disciplined body of men could have been found afloat. But affairs were about as usual, and war seemed no nearer than it had for the past five or six years. He was again in need of money, and as the pay of a captain in the service at this time was less than a hundred dollars a month, something had to be done, and, yielding to the strenuous advice of a number of his friends, he accepted a position once more in the merchant service and proceeded on a voyage to St. Petersburg.

When just inside the straits of the Baltic his vessel was captured by a Danish privateer and carried into Copenhagen. As luck would have it, he had not been at anchor more than a few minutes when who should come off to him in a small boat from the shore but his old friend Nissen, of Tripoli! The meeting between the two friends was cordial and their greetings more than hearty.

Nissen said that he had just happened to hear that the captured ship claimed to be an American, and some one who landed from the privateer had remembered Bainbridge's name. So at once he had hastened to tender his services.

"The very strangest coincidence, my dear sir," said Mr. Nissen, as he seated himself beside Bainbridge in the cabin, "is that this very day—aye, only an hour ago—I received the handsome urn which you and the rest of my kind friends, whom I had the pleasure of meeting when they were guests of the Bashaw, had sent me. It has only now arrived owing to the fact of our war with England."

"Yes, I remember," returned Bainbridge; "we ordered it of a London silversmith, and I trust that you will live long to possess it."

"Now, in regard to your being taken for an Englishman, and the mistake of your being brought in here," Nissen continued, "leave it all to me and do not worry."

In a few days Bainbridge parted from his old friend and went on to St. Petersburg, Nissen having completed all arrangements for his release.

His first voyage proving very successful, Bainbridge crossed the seas again to the same place. As he had been commissioned to undertake some valuable commercial negotiations, he determined to spend the winter at the capital, but hearing the news of the action that took place between his old command the frigate President and the English sloop-of-war Little Belt, he perceived at once that hostilities would surely follow, and throwing aside all his business responsibilities, he determined to report himself at Washington as soon as he possibly could.

During the winter the Baltic is closed to navigation and freezes over, and the only way for a traveler to reach the sea was by sledge overland through Sweden to Gothenburg. The story of this journey would make a long tale in itself. Bainbridge was placed under the protection of the Russian Government, and after various adventures and great suffering, which included a severe cold and injury received from falling over a precipice with his carriage—for he had traveled by sledge, rowboat, horseback, and coach in this journey—with great difficulty he arrived at his destination. On the 31st of December he set sail on a merchant vessel, after resting for eleven days in the harbor in company with a number of English men-of-war.

Bad fortune seemed to pursue him. Off the coast of Jutland three of the Englishmen were lost in a severe storm, and had it not been for the fact that Bainbridge obtained some influence over the commander of the vessel upon which he was a passenger, she too would undoubtedly have been lost. It was found necessary to put back to the coast of Norway.

On the 13th of January, 1812, the brig was again struck by a heavy gale while passing through the channel between the Orkneys and the Shetland Islands. The English captain, hearing the cries that there were breakers on the port bow, immediately began to sing out orders that Bainbridge, who was standing near him, perceived would cause the vessel to be upon the rocks. Without leave or permission, and before the crew had time to obey their captain, he had countermanded the latter's orders; and the man at the helm, remembering Bainbridge's action of a few days previous to this, kept the vessel on her course, with the result that the rocks were passed and danger averted.

After landing in England, Captain Bainbridge made all haste to Liverpool, stopping only for a visit to the American minister in London, to whom he delivered dispatches. On the 12th of February he arrived at New York, proceeding at once to Washington, where he reported himself ready for active service.

Congress was just at that moment deliberating on the subject of declaring war against Great Britain, and Bainbridge learned, to his great sorrow and chagrin, that in a Cabinet council it had been determined to lay up all our frigates and vessels of war in ordinary, it being thought better, forsooth, to save what little we had rather than risk losing our small force in action with the gigantic navy at the disposal of King George.

Bainbridge luckily met in Washington, Captain Charles Stewart, a brave fighter, and, after a consultation, he proposed that they should draw up a paper remonstrating strongly against the measure to the Secretary of the Navy. They rehearsed the consequences and the depressing effects of such action, and stated that the officers of the service would feel personally wronged if they were not permitted to at least court some of the dangers which their companions on land were facing. Altogether they made an able defense of their position, and the letter accomplished its purpose—the vessels were not laid up as had been intended.

Being assured that he had succeeded, much relieved, Bainbridge hastened to assume his post. He found the Charleston yard in a bad condition, but he at once began to make extensive changes, and to prepare for building a large naval station.

While in the midst of these operations the expected news was brought to him of the declaration of war that had been passed on the 18th of June, 1812, by the United States against Great Britain. A land post was not the place for a man of Bainbridge's disposition. At once he applied to be sent to sea, and requested that he be given command of one of the frigates soon to be in readiness. The Secretary of the Navy ordered him to the Constellation, and he was directed to proceed to Washington and fit her out with all dispatch.

Before long the Constellation was almost ready to go to sea, and Bainbridge returned to Charleston to make arrangements for leaving his family before going upon a cruise. He had been but three days in Boston when in sailed Hull in the Constitution, and the news of the victory over the Guerriere flew about the town.

Bainbridge hastened at once to meet with and congratulate his old friend, and there he, to his intense excitement, heard that Hull intended to remain on shore for a few months to attend to some private affairs.

The Constitution was then the pride of the navy. She was a better sailer and a finer ship in every way than the Constellation; and as soon as Bainbridge found that Hull intended to give her up, he applied to Secretary Hamilton for the command of her. His request was granted, and, to his delight, Bainbridge found that he had been appointed to the command of a small squadron of three vessels, consisting of his own vessel, the Hornet under the command of his old shipmate Lawrence, and the Essex under the command of Porter, who had suffered in Tripoli with him. A rendezvous was appointed, and on the fifteenth day of September, 1812, Bainbridge flew his first blue pennant. Porter, who was then at anchor in the Delaware, was directed to set sail for the Cape Verd Islands, stop at Porto Praya, a bay in the island of Santiago, and from whence he was to proceed to the island of Fernando de Noronha. And if the Essex did not meet with the Constitution and Hornet at the last-named port, Porter was ordered to touch at the island of St. Catherine, and if unsuccessful, cruise to the southward, his only orders being to use judgment and to annoy the enemy's commerce.

It was the 26th of October when the Constitution and Hornet sailed from Boston together. Fair weather was met with, and the two vessels reached Fernando de Noronha early in December. For some time they waited hoping that the Essex would join them. The island is a penal colony of Portugal; it was not a pleasant anchorage, nor was their position exactly agreeable to Bainbridge, for he was compelled to sail under false colors, something distasteful to his nature. The Portuguese Government was then in league with Great Britain, and both the Constitution and the Hornet flew the English flag. Bainbridge was representing himself as Captain Kerr of his Majesty's ship Acasta of forty-four guns, and the Hornet pretended to be the Morgiana of twenty guns.

It was impossible to obtain a supply of fresh water at this place, and so Bainbridge determined to sail away, leaving a letter addressed to "Sir James Yeo," which was the name agreed upon that Porter would take if he stopped at the island. Bainbridge bade farewell to the Governor and made off for San Salvador.

Although Commandant Porter received the missive left for him, and followed out the instructions contained

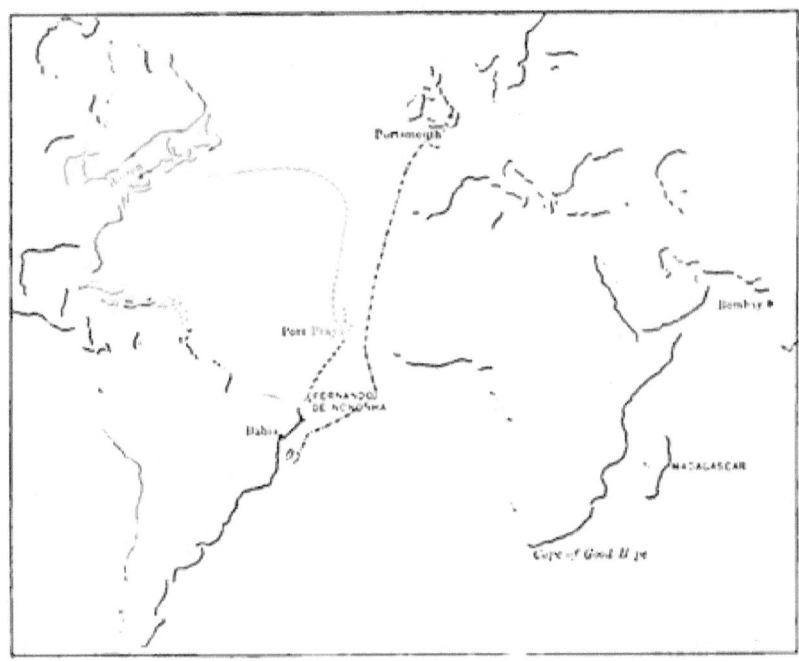

Cruise of the Constitution, Hornet and Java.

therein, he did not have the fortune of running across his superior officer, and following the dictates of his own judgment, he sailed on that remarkable cruise into the waters of the Pacific.

Captain Lawrence entered the harbor of San Salvador leaving the Constitution anchored at the entrance. His instructions were to ascertain through the United States consul the disposition of the Government of Brazil toward the United States, and also to find out if there were any

British cruisers on the coast, and what chance there was of picking up a British merchantman. He had not landed from his vessel when he saw under the lee of a small island in the inner harbor a fine, loftily sparred sloop of war of a few more tons burden than his own, but not large enough to frighten him. Asking who she was, he was informed that it was his Majesty's corvette Bonne Citoyenne, the "Good Citizeness," and Mr. Hill, the American consul, informed him confidentially that the English ship was laden with specie and had been ready to sail for two or three days, her destiny being England.

When Lawrence had an opportunity to speak to Bainbridge he informed him joyfully of the news, and requested permission to use every means to bring off an action between the Hornet and the English vessel.

Bainbridge gave his consent at once, and eagerly Lawrence made preparations for the action that he thought was surely to take place. The next day Bainbridge, thinking, perhaps, it would be an inducement for the Bonne Citoyenne to leave her anchorage and come out and fight, sailed away, and Lawrence immediately sent the following communication in to Consul Hill:

"When last I saw you I stated my wishes to meet the Bonne Citoyenne, and authorized you to make it known to Captain Green. I now request you to state to him, and pledge my honor, that neither the Constitution nor any other American vessel will interfere."

CHAPTER XVIII.

The British consul without delay transmitted the communication he had received from Consul Hill to Captain Green, but the English officer proved to be a very prudent man indeed, for he replied that while he did not doubt that he would be successful should a combat take place between his own vessel and the Hornet, he really doubted that Commodore Bainbridge would abstain from taking a hand, for the reason that the " Paramount duty which he (Bainbridge) owes to his country would prevent him from becoming an inactive spectator and seeing a ship belonging to the very squadron under his orders fall into the hands of the enemy."

When the American consul had read Captain Green's reason for not wishing to meet Lawrence, he wrote immediately to his British friend, stating that Bainbridge had given assurance that he would confirm Captain Lawrence's statement, making use of the following words: " If Captain Green wishes to try equal force, I pledge my honor to give him an opportunity by being out of the way or not interfering."

Nevertheless, Green kept the harbor, and Lawrence assiduously blockaded him. The Governor of Bahia, Count d'Arcos, had displayed a very unfriendly attitude toward the United States, and objected to the Hornet's anchoring in the harbor. Bainbridge, hearing of this and waxing wroth, as soon as he returned wrote a strong letter of remonstrance to the count, and then again he set out alone in the Constitution after sending the following order to the waiting Lawrence: "I shall keep off the land to the northward of latitude 12° 20″, when you will meet me there, except you have great reason to believe the Bonne Citoyenne is coming out. In that case watch close and join me on Saturday next. May glory and success attend you."

This was the morning of the 26th of December, and three days later Bainbridge found the chance that he had so long been waiting for.

It was 9 A. M., with a fine sailing breeze blowing, and the shore of Brazil bore about ten leagues off on the

Bahia.

port hand when two sails were sighted on the weather bow. They were very distant, and it took over an hour's sailing to determine their character. Then Lieutenant Aylwin reported to the cabin that the strangers were evidently large ships, and as the Constitution approached they parted company; one stood on to meet her, and the other made in to the land.

Lieutenant Parker, of the Constitution, at first thought that the approaching vessel might be the Essex, but Bainbridge, after a careful look through the glass declared her to be British, and at eleven o'clock he tacked to the southward and eastward, hauling up his mainsail and taking in his royals in order to give the stranger an opportunity to draw nigh. In half an hour he made the private signal for the day, and perceiving that it was not answered, he immediately set his mainsails and royals again, and made preparations to get out his studding sails. Observing one of the officers cast a curious look up aloft, Bainbridge turned and spoke to him laughingly:

"It was merely to draw our friend off the coast and away from his consort," indicating the ship well inshore "We will be exchanging compliments," he added, "in two hours or less, and I hope that before sundown we will have given a good account of ourselves." And by sundown indeed they had.

Probably the commander of the English frigate, for such she had now proved herself beyond a doubt, supposed that the American (the Constitution had flown her flag for an hour before it was answered) wished to escape him. But if this was his idea he was soon deprived of it.

"Shorten sail, Mr. Parker," said Bainbridge quietly. "We'll tack ship in about ten minutes. Clear decks for action, sir!"

It was a grand sight to see these two fine frigates approaching one another. The day was bright, their colors shone, and the crews were standing at the guns stripped to the waist. The sanded decks and the grim tables laid out below in the cockpit were notes that were entirely out of accord with Nature's aspect. There was an anxious moment when it seemed that the other vessel wished to avoid a meeting. But it was soon seen that this was but a feint; the oncoming Britisher, who now had a flag flying at her peak and mizzenmast-head, intended raking. The Constitution wore, and cleverly avoided her.

"Well that's a strange thing!" remarked Lieutenant Aylwin who had been a midshipman on board the Constitution in her fight with the Guerrière. "See, she has lowered all her flags except the jack at the mizzenmast-head!" He glanced aloft at the spars of his own ship.

From every masthead, from the peak, and from two places in the shrouds, fluttered the Stars and Stripes. Nearer the two frigates approached in dead silence. It was generally customary for vessels of the American and English service to go into action cheering; but no one seemed disposed to lead off on the Constitution—it was too early in the game.

At 2 P. M. the distance between the ships was less than half a mile. Bainbridge sent an order to the officer in charge of the third division, ordering him to fire a gun ahead of the enemy, in order to make him show his colors. No sooner was this done than the Englishman replied with a broadside, and ran his flag up to the peak again.

For fully five minutes the Constitution did not reply; but when she had her antagonist, who was well to leeward, within grapeshot distance she began the action in earnest, and in the first few exchanges it appeared that matters were going hard indeed, for she appeared to have the worst of it. Bainbridge was talking to Lieutenant Parker, when suddenly the latter saw him flinch and drop his hand to his side. But he continued the conversation, remarking the good effect of the Constitution's gunnery upon the enemy.

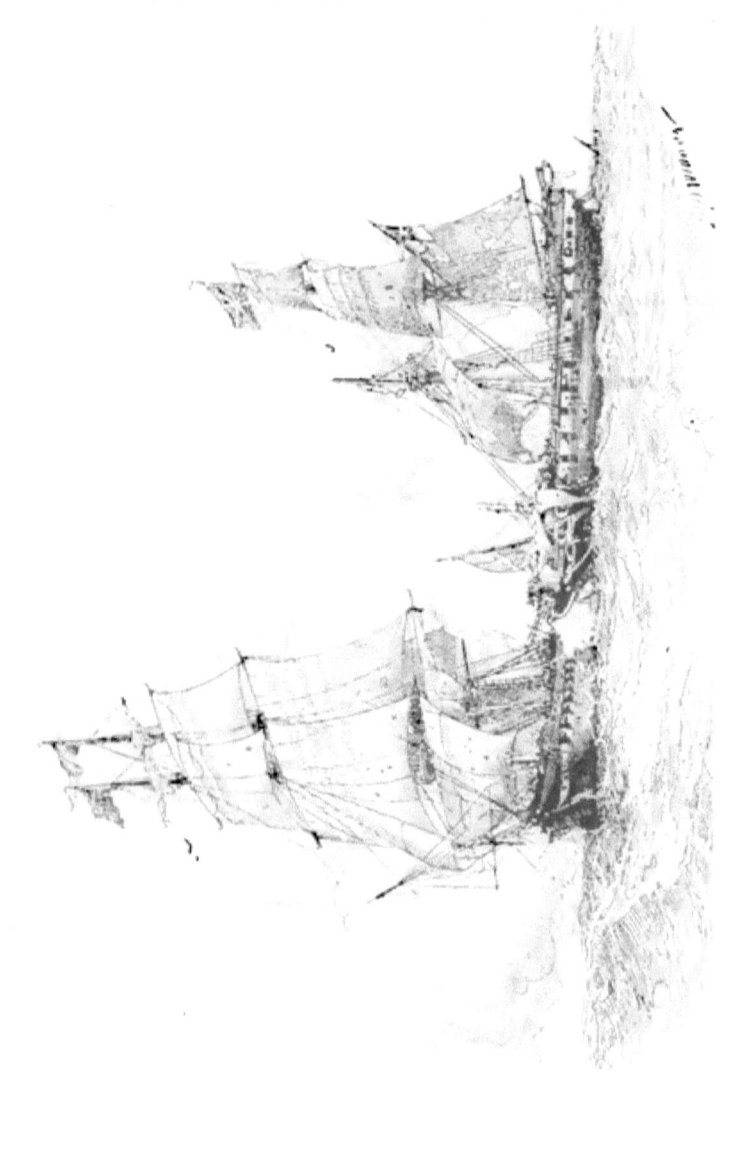

"You are wounded, Captain Bainbridge!" exclaimed the lieutenant, suddenly glancing down.

Bainbridge was pressing his hand tightly against his hip.

"It's nothing," he said; "at least 'tis not dangerous, I'm sure. Call no attention to it, sir!" There was the ring of an order and not an entreaty in his words.

Parker saluted and said nothing further. At this moment a round shot from one of the enemy's after guns entered a port, struck the breech of one of the carronades, and then bounded like lightning across the deck. In a second the air was full of splinters. They rose like a cloud of dry dust. Bainbridge and the officers on the quarter-deck hurried forward to see what damage had been done. The wheel had been shot away completely! The quartermaster and the seamen who were at the spokes were lying badly wounded on the deck. At first glance this loss would have seemed quite irreparable.

"There's more than one way to steer a ship!" Bainbridge exclaimed. "Order eight men down into the after hold, and station three midshipmen on the after companion ladders to pass the word."

During the rest of the engagement the Constitution was handled by means of steering tackles from below.

The way her guns were now replying to the constant fire of the English frigate delighted Bainbridge's heart. They were served with precision and trained with accuracy, and as he attempted to close, the Englishman's jib boom was shot away, then the bowsprit, and at five minutes past three down came his foremast by the board! Only a few minutes before this happened the Constitution had crossed her antagonist's bows so close as to foul her mizzen rigging.

Bainbridge had again been wounded, this time by a copper bolt, which was driven with great force into his thigh; but he would not leave the deck, and scarcely would he permit the surgeon to attend to him, so engrossed was he in handling ship.

It would take a seaman's knowledge to follow the various manœuvres of the latter part of the action. Bainbridge's journal speaks of the succession of incidents in the following laconic fashion: " It was five minutes past three when the enemy's foremast was shot away. At fifteen minutes past three, shot away his main-topmast just above the cap. At forty minutes past three, shot away the gaff and spanker boom. At fifty-five minutes past three, shot away his mizzenmast nearly by the board. At five minutes past four, having silenced the fire of the enemy completely, and the colors in his main rigging being down, we supposed that he had struck. We then hauled down our courses and shot ahead to repair our rigging, which was extremely cut, leaving the enemy a complete wreck; soon afterward discovered that the enemy's flag was still flying. Hove to to repair some of our damage. At twenty minutes past four, wore ship and stood for the enemy. At twenty-five minutes past five, got very close in a very effectual raking position athwart his bows, and when about to fire he most prudently struck his flag, for had he suffered the broadside to have raked him his additional loss must have been extremely great as he lay an unmanageable wreck upon the water."

As soon as it was seen that the English frigate was a prize, the Constitution's crew broke out into loud and continued cheering. Bainbridge turned to Lieutenant Parker with a smile of satisfaction and ordered him to lower away the first cutter, which was the only boat capable of floating. Soon she was alongside, and her crew tumbled into her most eagerly.

It was seven o'clock when Lieutenant Parker returned, bringing with him Lieutenant Chads, first of his Majesty's thirty-eight-gun frigate Java; Lieutenant-General Hislop, Governor of Bombay; and Major Walker and Captain Wood, of his staff. Lieutenant Chads, who was slightly wounded, brought the message that his commander was too badly hurt to be moved. Hearing that the loss of life on board the Java had been extremely great, and taking into account the complete wreck to which she had been reduced, every exertion was now made for transferring the prisoners and wounded, for it was determined to destroy her instead of trying to bring her into port.

The wounded Captain Lambert was brought over and placed in Bainbridge's own cabin, and everything was done to alleviate his sufferings. Despite his own painful wounds, the American captain did not leave the deck until after eleven o'clock on the night of the engagement.

There has been not a little controversy in regard to the numbers engaged in the action on both sides. The Constitution was undoubtedly the superior in the number of guns and men. She carried fifty-four guns and four hundred and eighty men composed her crew, of whom nine were killed and twenty-five wounded. The Java, despite her rating as a thirty-eight, carried forty-seven guns and four hundred and twenty-six men, out of which she lost sixty killed and one hundred and one wounded.

The next morning the Java was blown up, and the Constitution was so little injured that she was in readiness to begin another action if it were necessary. Both captains were now dangerously ill, and poor young Lieutenant Aylwin had died from severe wounds only a few hours after the Java had struck her flag. Under Bainbridge's direction everything was done that could possibly help to the comfort of the wounded prisoners, and it was decided to land them all under parole at Bahia.

Just before the landing, when the English captain was

brought up on deck. Bainbridge, supported by surgeon Evans and Lieutenant Shubrick, approached the cot upon which Lambert lay. Placing the sword that had been surrendered to him beside the suffering man, he leaned over him, and with great emotion spoke as follows:

"I return your sword, my dear sir, with my sincerest wish that you will recover and wear it, as you have hitherto done, with honor to yourself and to your country."

Lambert murmured his thanks, and grasped Bainbridge's hand in his feeble fingers.

General Hislop presented to Bainbridge a handsome sword, not in surrender, but in token of gratitude for his conduct and treatment of those unfortunates whom the fate of war had placed in his keeping.

The cordial relations established between Bainbridge and the Governor General were of a lasting character, and the latter was always proud to speak of the American captain as his friend.

When the Constitution arrived off San Salvador she found the little Hornet still maintaining the blockade of the port, and there Bainbridge left her. As the Essex had failed to keep her rendezvous, he deemed it best to return to the United States, and so he set sail on the 6th of January, 1813. On the 27th of the following month he arrived in Boston, and from a paper published two days after his arrival the following extract is taken:

Sword presented to Bainbridge by Gen. Hislop of the Java.

Bainbridge's reception at Boston.

"Captain Bainbridge landed at the Long Wharf amid loud acclamations and roaring of the cannon from the shore. All the way from the end of the pier to the Exchange Coffee House was decorated with colors and streamers.

A procession was formed in Faneuil Hall by Major Tilden and was escorted by the Boston Light Infantry and the Winslow Blues. Decorations and streamers were strung across State Street, while the windows and the tops of the houses were filled with spectators. Captain Bainbridge was distinguished by his noble figure and by his walking uncovered. On his right hand was the veteran Captain Rodgers, and on his left Brigadier-General Welles; then followed the brave Captain Hull, Colonel Blake, and a number of officers and citizens. But the crowd was so immense that it was difficult to keep the order of the processions. The band of music in the balcony of the State Bank and the music of the New England Guards had a fine effect.

On the 2d of March a splendid public dinner was given in the Exchange Coffee House to Captain Bainbridge and his officers. The procession was formed at Faneuil Hall and was escorted amid the applause of the citizens by a battalion composed of the Boston Light Infantry and the Winslow Blues, commanded by Colonel Sargeant. Before sitting down to the table the blessing of Almighty God was asked in a most impressive manner by the Rev. Mr. Holley."

Although the victory over the Java was the culminating deed of Commodore Bainbridge's career, he lived to serve his country longer, and the results of his good judgment and nautical skill in the building of navy-yard docks and in the revision of the signal code were of great value to the service.

From his example many young officers profited, and

from the teachings of his life those now living can learn the proper meaning of patriotism. His last words, spoken in delirium, were an index to his character. "Call all hands," cried he, rising in his bed, "and prepare to board the enemy!"

THE END.

www.ingramcontent.com/pod-product-compliance
Lightning Source LLC
Chambersburg PA
CBHW020241170426

43202CB00008B/177